ECHOES OF AFRICATOWN

"FOOTPRINTS OF THE ENSLAVED"
AUTHOR & POET.
FM. NICKSON
Inspired by historical accounts.

Echoes of Africatown: "Footprints of the ensalved"

FM Nickson

Published by FM Nickson, 2023.

---

1. http://www.fmnickson.com

Table of Contents

From the Author

1. *3050 (The Last Sanctuary)*
2. *Whispers of the Heart- Timeless poetry*

To all avid readers,

May this book serve as a captivating and thought-provoking tale that transports you to different worlds, inspires you to reflect on history and the complexities of human nature, and entertains you with its rich storytelling. I hope that you enjoy the journey through the pages of this novel, and that it leaves a lasting impression on you.

DEDICATION

To all those whose lives have been touched by the injustice and trauma of slavery, this book serves as a reminder of the resilience and strength of the human spirit; to honor the memory of those who suffered and strive to create a world that values and respects the dignity and worth of every person.

To those who have stood and continue to stand against the evils of slavery, racism, and discrimination, this book is dedicated to you. Your tireless efforts in promoting equality and justice have paved the way for a better future for all. May your unwavering commitment to this cause inspire future generations to continue the fight for a world free of oppression and bigotry.

To my amiable Daughter Myra Makena and beloved Son Nathaniel Taifa, there is always a place for you in the world. Find it and leave an impact. If you ever feel small, remember we're all just a speck of dust in the universe. Our lives are so small in the grand scheme of things, but also know that every life, no matter how small, has the power to make a difference. We might be tiny specks in the universe, but we have the ability to shine bright and leave a lasting impact on the world.

With love and gratitude.
[fm. nickson]

PREFACE

Exploring the history of slavery and its impact on African Americans is a complex and sensitive undertaking. As the author of this book, I have approached this subject matter with great care and respect for those who endured this traumatic experience. Through extensive research, I have endeavored to present a possible account of the events that occurred, through the lens of a descendant of the last slave ship to enter the United States, albeit in a fictional setup.

It is my fervent hope that this book will cast light on a pivotal, yet oft-neglected period in American history, and encourage readers to dive deeper into the events that unfolded just 160 years ago in Africatown, Alabama, United States.

The events and characters in this book have been fashioned by the author to serve as narrators, and to bring to life the real people who were affected by the events that took place in Africatown, and the appalling history of slavery that commenced in Alabama, many decades ago.

Africatown, also known as Plateau, is a historic neighborhood located in *Mobile County, Alabama, USA*. The community was founded by a group of enslaved Africans who were brought to the United States on the last known slave ship, famously referred to as The *Clotilda*, in 1860. After the Civil War and emancipation, the community formed a distinct identity and culture, maintaining their African traditions and creating their own social institutions. The community was named after Africa, the continent of origin of *The Clotilda* captives. The settlers were able to purchase land in the area after the Civil War and formed the community of Africatown after realizing there was never going back to Africa. They had to build their own Africa in the United States.

They established their own church, school, and social clubs, and preserved their culture through music, dance, and oral traditions. The community has continued to preserve its history and culture through the efforts of local activists, historians, and community leaders. Today, Africatown is a symbol of resilience and cultural heritage, with many efforts underway to preserve and promote its history.

The *Africatown Welcome Center and Museum* serves as a hub for the community's cultural and educational programs, and at the time of writing this book, efforts were underway to develop the area into a cultural heritage tourism destination. One of the most significant events in Africatown's history was the discovery of *The Clotilda* in 2019, the very slave ship that was forever lost in history.

Journalist Ben Raines made the historic discovery, locating The Clotilda on the riverbed of Mobile River Bay in Atlantic, Alabama, over a century after it was scuttled and sank. This discovery provided further evidence that the individuals who established a settlement in Africatown after emancipation were forcibly brought to the United States in an illegal and non-consensual manner, and that the ship that transported them was intentionally set ablaze and sunk in the Mobile River to conceal evidence of this abhorrent practice.

The history of Africatown is a poignant and intriguing account of a group of individuals who were brought to the United States against their will and the obstacles they overcame to establish a life for themselves and their descendants.

Presently, Black Americans and descendants of *The Clotilda* survivors, journey to Africa annually, searching for answers about their ancestral lineage. For many, it is a deeply emotional expedition, allowing them to reconnect with their past and rediscover the land of their forefathers.

The pilgrimage to Africa thus for the descendants of The Clotilda and Africatown and other Black Americans is not merely a physical undertaking but a spiritual one as well. It presents an opportunity for them to pay homage to their ancestors, gain knowledge of their history and culture, and create connections with the thriving communities in the lands where their forefathers were abducted from.

To those with a profound understanding of the understated slave trade that ceased only about 162 years ago in the United States, I extend a figurative pat on the back. For the uninitiated, allow me to provide a brief overview.

Africatown is the dwelling place of descendants of the last slave ship to berth in the country in July 1860. This vessel, famously known as *The Clotilda,* brought over 100 "human cargo", including men, women, and children, from the Dahomey Kingdom in West Africa, present day Benin.

Congress had prohibited the United States' involvement in the Atlantic slave trade through the Act Prohibiting importation of Slaves, which took effect on January 1, 1808, but this did not stop the illicit trade. The illegal trade in human beings continued, buoyed by avarice and the ever-growing demand for labor in the cotton fields of the South. One individual, *Timothy Meaher,* challenged wealthy plantation owners in Alabama, boasting that he could still import slaves into the country despite the law. He made good on his word, dispatching *Captain William Foster* to West Africa in March 1860, where he acquired and loaded the "human cargo" onto *The Clotilda* slave ship for a grueling six-week voyage to Alabama.

The passage of *The Clotilda* was marked by unimaginable suffering, as over one hundred people, including men, women, and children, were crammed into the vessel's cramped quarters for an arduous six-week voyage across the tumultuous Atlantic Ocean. Eventually, in May of 1860, the ship would arrive in Mobile Bay, Alabama, and about 110 African individuals would survive the ordeal. Once the vessel docked, *Timothy Meaher,* who had orchestrated the illegal slave trade, ordered the ship to be destroyed and sunk in the Mobile river, hoping to cover up his misdeeds. Some of the enslaved individuals were sold into forced labor in Southern cotton plantations, while Meaher kept the rest to work on his own plantation. Following the Emancipation Proclamation of 1865, the slaves were technically free, but faced a future without homes, land, or direction. Many desired to return to Africa, but the journey was both costly and perilous. In response, they united to purchase land from their enslavers in Alabama, forming a new community, which they named **Africatown.** The story of *The Clotilda* is one of immense tragedy and pain, as a group of innocent individuals was torn from their homeland and forced into a life of servitude. Despite the horrors they faced however, their resilience and determination to build a new life for themselves and their descendants have left a lasting legacy that continues to inspire today.

The quest to find the submerged wreckage of *The Clotilda* proved to be an arduous task, with numerous efforts falling short over the years. The ship's watery grave appeared to be guarding its dark secrets from prying eyes. However, in May 2019, after years of persistent searching, *The Clotilda* was finally discovered by one brave journalist *Ben Raines*, and the Alabama Historical Commission verified its identity. The site was subsequently added to the National Register of Historic Places in 2021, serving as a poignant reminder of the gravest offense ever perpetrated against humanity. While the discovery of The Clotilda was undoubtedly a momentous occasion, it also rekindled a flood of painful memories and emotions for three distinct groups: the descendants of those who were forced into slavery, the descendants of the fellow Africans who sold them, and the descendants of their American enslavers. This leads us to ponder what justice might look like more than a century and a half after *The Clotilda's* brazen and illicit voyage.

For *Kamau Sadiki,* a member of the Smithsonian Slave Wrecks Project and a diver who explored the sunken remains of the ship, the experience was deeply moving. The anguish and agony, the shrieks and cries of those who were confined within its hold, echoed within him, and he needed to pause briefly to compose himself.

"The discovery of the Clotilda, nearly 160 years after it was burned, and the possibility that descendants of the enslaved may have been living nearby all along, underscores how much of American history remains untold, how many stories remain unknown." - *Bryan Stevenson, founder and executive director of the Equal Justice Initiative.*

"The story of Africatown is a testament to the resilience of the human spirit and a reminder of the sacrifices made by those who came before us." - *Senator Doug Jones, who introduced a bill in 2019 to establish The Clotilda National Historical Park.*

"The Clotilda is a powerful symbol of our nation's ongoing struggle with race and inequality, and the story of Africatown highlights the resilience of the human spirit in the face of oppression and adversity." - *Lonnie Bunch, founding director of the National Museum of African American History and Culture.*

"The discovery of the Clotilda and the establishment of the Africatown community are important reminders of the painful legacy of slavery in our country, and they should serve as a call to action for all of us to work towards a more just and equitable future." - *Stacey Abrams, political activist and former Georgia gubernatorial candidate.*

"Africatown is a living testament to the strength, resilience, and courage of the human spirit in the face of adversity." - *Hank Aaron, baseball legend and native of Mobile, Alabama.*

"Footprints of the Enslaved"

Despite the law, the trade persisted
Driven by greed, the demand existed
A man named Meaher made a daring bet
To bring slaves, and not be caught yet.
The Clotilda was the ship that he chose
A vessel that would bring much woes
Over one hundred Africans it smuggled in
Their future uncertain, their lives in a spin.
These people were brought to a place unknown
Their lives up-rooted, their families left alone
Taken from their homes, their land and their kin
Captured in chains, a brutal journey to begin.
The voyage was long, the journey was cruel
Their captors were heartless,
their future burnt in the ship's fuel
They yearned for freedom,
a chance to be free
But alas, their fate was not theirs to decree.
Their arrival was not the end of their plight
Forced to work, from morning till night
In the cotton fields of the Southern State
Their fate sealed, their dreams to emancipate.
But through their hardships and endless pain
Held onto hope, persevered through the strain
Their descendants live on, their legacy strong
Their spirit unbroken, their resilience a song.

"ECHOES OF AFRICATOWN"

A glimpse into a dark and gruesome history
"Footprints of The Enslaved"

Echoes of Africatown is a powerful literary work that will transport readers into the depths of the slave trade and the indomitable spirit of a people who refused to be broken. Through the perspective of **Tusoli**, a fictional character, this gripping novel recounts the heart-wrenching journey of the last slave ship to dock in the United States and the stories of the descendants who still call Africatown home.

As readers walk in the character's footsteps, tracing the same paths as her ancestors, they'll be immersed in the raw emotion and power of a history that has long been buried. From the brutal capture of the enslaved people in the Dahomey Kingdom to the audacious voyage of *The Clotilda* and the merciless treatment they faced upon arrival, the novel offers a unique window into a world that has remained hidden for far too long. But amidst the pain and suffering, *Echoes of Africatown* also reveals the unyielding spirit of a people who refused to be defeated.

The novel is a Tribute to the strength and determination of those who rebuilt Africatown from the ashes of their past and who continue to honor their heritage and traditions to this day. As the pages turn, readers will gain a deeper understanding of the atrocities of the past and a newfound appreciation for the courage and resilience of those who fought to survive. *Echoes of Africatown* is more than a book; it is an unforgettable expedition into the heart and soul of a people who refused to be silenced.

Torn between the love she has for her fiancé, Jonathan, who just proposed to her, and a deep-seated desire to uncover her roots, Tusoli embarks on a journey of discovery. Born and raised in Africatown, she graduated with a degree in medicine and got a job as a doctor in Auburn, a city in Alabama. But everything takes a dramatic turn that fuels her quest to rediscover her roots and explore the history of her ancestors. Her quest for self-discovery took her on an exhilarating adventure that spanned continents and oceans.

As she probed into the history of her forefathers, Tusoli encountered a world that was both haunting and beautiful, where the past collided with the present, and the lasting impact of slavery reverberated in every corner. From the bustling markets of Zanzibar to the desolate plains of Kenya, Tusoli's journey takes her through a kaleidoscope of cultures, traditions, and landscapes. She meets people from all walks of life; from Masai warriors to coastal fishermen, and each encounter deepens her understanding of her own history and heritage.

Tusoli's journey wasn't just a quest for knowledge; it was a quest for redemption. As she came to terms with the trauma of her past and confronted the demons that had haunted her for so long, she began to see the world in a new light. She discovered that love and forgiveness could heal even the deepest wounds and that the strength of the human spirit was truly limitless. Despite the moments of hope and solace she encounters during her journey, Tusoli remains mindful of the agonizing pain and affliction her forefathers and mothers endured. When she finally stands at the ***Door of No Return*** in Benin, west Africa, she feels their voices echoing in her soul, a reminder of the horrors of slavery and the need to never forget.

Throughout her odyssey, she meets Leonardo, an intrepid and charismatic voyager who captures her affections. But will she let love sidetrack her from her goal of self-discovery, or will she stay true to her resolve of unearthing her ancestry? Embark on an extraordinary expedition of personal growth and reconciliation with Tusoli; an expedition that will take you from one end of Africa to the other, and indelibly transform you.

Author: FM. Nickson

DAUGHTER OF AFRICA

In a land where the sun sets like fire,
And the savanna stretches far and wide,
There is a beauty that never tires,
A queen that leaves you in awe and pride.
Her skin is the shade of ebony,
Her eyes the color of warm honey,
Her lips full and luscious as peach,
Her curves a perfectionist' stitch.
She moves with the grace of a gazelle,
And her voice is as sweet as a bird's trill,
Her laughter brings light to the darkest spell,
And her presence commands attention still.
For she is not just a woman, but a queen,
A daughter of Africa, a regal being,
With a spirit as fierce as the Serengeti,
And a heart as pure as the Nile's stream.
She embodies the strength of a lioness,
And the wisdom of an ancient goddess,
Her aura radiates with passion and love,
And her soul sings like a soaring dove.
She is a symbol of power and resilience,
And her beauty is beyond mere appearance,
For she represents the heart of Africa,
A land of wonders, a continent of grandeur.

She is the African Queen,
A gem to behold, a sight to be seen,
And in her presence, one cannot but glean,
The magic and majesty of this land, so serene.
Her soul sings with the rhythms of the drums
Her feet dance to the beat of the earth
She is the Daughter of Africa, and she hums
A melody that gives her people mirth.
If you ever see her passing by
With her head held high and her smile bright
Remember that she carries a history nigh
And her spirit shines with a powerful light.

CHAPTER 1
FAMILY TRADITION

As the golden orb of the Sun descended below the horizon, and the clock chimed six in the tranquil hamlet of Africatown, Helena bustled around the kitchen, applying the final flourishes to an extraordinary feast she had prepared for her daughter Tusoli. This was no ordinary day, for it marked a triumvirate of momentous occasions in Tusoli's life. Firstly, it was her birthday, a day of celebration and joy. Secondly, tomorrow would witness the culmination of seven long years of rigorous toil, as Tusoli would finally be graduating from medical school. Yet, on this day, there was another family ritual that demanded its due; a tradition that had been handed down across generations.

Helena watched her daughter extinguish the flickering flames atop her birthday cake, and a surge of pride and emotion engulfed her. The decision to bestow the sacred family ritual upon her daughter had been a heavy one, causing her to vacillate for days on end. Yet, as the words of her own mother echoed in her mind, "One without knowledge of their history is akin to a wild tree bereft of roots," Helena was resolute in her determination to honor the tradition.

With veneration, Helena strode towards her bedroom and retrieved a petite wooden box that had remained unopened for no less than three decades. Tenderly setting it on the meticulously adorned dining table, she was inundated with a gamut of emotions- pride, nostalgia, and a hint of sorrow. The wooden box that lay before her was a precious family heirloom, one that had been cherished and passed down through many generations, and as her late mother had requested, Helena had made a solemn vow to uphold the family tradition, and now her moment had finally come. It was her sacred duty to pass the cherished box to her daughter, Tusoli, just as it had been lovingly entrusted to her by her own mother. This rite of passage, steeped in generations of history and emotion, carried the weight of countless memories and promises fulfilled.

It was a pivotal moment in the family's history, and Helena was determined to ensure that the legacy endured for many more generations. The vintage wooden box, though outwardly unassuming, held within it a glimpse into a dark and gruesome past—a harrowing account of the disorienting trauma of slavery that had plagued their family for generations. Inhaling deeply, Helena centered herself, ready to narrate the story to Tusoli and bestow upon her the sacred box. With resolute bearing, she prepared to share their family's history, ensuring that the tradition remained cherished and continued to be passed down long after Tusoli's time.

The coastal village of Shimoni, nestled on the southern coast of Kenya, may seem like an idyllic destination for tourists seeking adventure and relaxation in Africa. However, beneath the picturesque scenery and sun-kissed beaches, lies a dark and harrowing past, embodied by an ancient cave that had become a symbol of human suffering and tragedy. As the waves of the Indian Ocean relentlessly crash against the rocky shore, the cave stands as a testament to the brutal history of the slave trade that happened many centuries ago. It is said that countless men, women, and children were forcibly taken from their homes and herded into this eerie cave, where they awaited their unknown fate. The cramped and confined space was a stark contrast to the open skies and vast savannas that these unfortunate souls had once known as home.

The cave's mystique lies not only in its foreboding depths but in the story it tells. The unmarked graves of those who perished within its walls are a haunting reminder of the atrocities committed during the slave trade era. Even today, the cave serves as a poignant symbol of the many lives that were lost and the unimaginable suffering that was inflicted upon them. It is a reminder that the wounds of history, while they may have faded, have not yet healed. For those who dare to venture into its depths, the cave offers a sobering and emotional experience. It is a powerful reminder of the collective responsibility that we all share to ensure that such horrors never happen again. The story of this cave, and others like it, must be told and retold to ensure that the lessons of history are never forgotten.

Today, the caves represent a fascinating historical gem that goes back many centuries. The history of the Shimoni caves is a haunting reminder of the gruesome realities of the transatlantic slave trade. For many years, these ancient caves served as a holding pen for millions of slaves before they were shipped to the slave markets, depriving Africa of its healthiest and most able men and women at the time.

According to historical accounts, the enslaved people were held captive in the Shimoni caves for a period of two to three weeks, subjected to inhumane conditions as they awaited their unknown fate. Upon the arrival of the slave ships, up to a thousand individuals were crammed into the ship's holds with little regard for their health or well-being. The journey across the ocean was fraught with danger, as many perished from disease, starvation, and mistreatment during the perilous voyage. Tragically, it is believed that many of the slaves who were transported across the Atlantic did not survive the journey and were discarded overboard like inanimate objects.

The year is 1857, and a ship looms large at the mouth of the Shimoni caves, its silhouette stark against the setting sun. After enduring almost three weeks of confinement in the damp and oppressive cave, the enslaved men, women, and children emerge, their faces etched with fear and resignation. Shackled and huddled in line together, they await their fate, their eyes reflecting the uncertainty of what lies ahead. The captain's voice echoes over the rocky cliffs as he counts, his words a grim reminder of their dehumanizing journey—approximately eight hundred souls now bound for the treacherous voyage across the Atlantic. The ship, a looming specter of exploitation, stands ready to transport this tragic cargo to distant shores, where they will be sold into a life of forced labor, their identities reduced to mere commodities in the eyes of their captors.

More than twenty days had passed since their departure from the shores, and the voyage had proven to be nothing short of harrowing. Tragically, the situation was compounded by an insidious contagion that swept through the vessel, a grim consequence of the deplorable conditions in which the slaves were forced to endure. The cramped quarters offered scant relief, with ceilings barely surpassing four feet in height, leaving the hapless captives no choice but to suffer in squalor. In such dire circumstances, they were left with no option but to defecate where they lay or sat, adding to the misery of their already unbearable existence.

The sweltering heat, in conjunction with the absence of any proper ventilation, only served to exacerbate the spread of the malady, rendering their circumstances nearly unbearable. As the contagion mercilessly ravaged the unfortunate captives, those too weak to withstand its cruel grip succumbed to their fate, their bodies tossed callously overboard into the unforgiving sea. Each splash a grim testament to the horrors of their journey, lost to the depths with no ceremony or recognition of their humanity.

During the voyage, just after a treacherous sort of calm, the water began to oscillate. As the ocean roiled and churned, it suddenly erupted into a violent frenzy hurling the vessel and its occupants to and fro amidst towering waves and deep troughs. A fierce storm swept in from the south, its powerful winds reigning over the frothing peaks like an ancient monarch. The vessel's once orderly deck was now a scene of pandemonium, as the tempest unleashed its fury. The tumultuous waves crashed against the sides of the vessel, sending it lurching violently, while the crew, already struggling to maintain control, found themselves overwhelmed by the sheer ferocity of the storm.

The slaves, confined to their cramped quarters, were at the mercy of the elements, and the relentless fury of the tempest shattered their confines, unleashing a torrent of water that claimed many lives. Those who survived were left traumatized and adrift, their spirits broken by the unforgiving sea. Meanwhile, the crew, bewildered and enraged, grappled with the devastating loss, struggling to comprehend the magnitude of the tragedy that had unfolded before their eyes.

In the wake of the tempest's havoc, Abisai, a resourceful slave, surveyed the wreckage with a shrewd eye and discerned a startling truth: only two of their captors' crew remained alive. With quick-witted cunning, he devised a daring scheme to wrest control of the vessel from the weakened crew, ensuring that they would not be condemned to face the perils of the treacherous Atlantic waters any longer. Guided by his unwavering determination, Abisai rallied his fellow slaves, and together they overpowered the incapacitated crew, seizing the reins of the ship. Through sheer force of will, they steered the beleaguered vessel towards the nearest shoreline, a distant hope on the horizon. Their arduous journey led them to the shores of present-day Mozambique, where they triumphantly broke free from the shackles of their oppressors and claimed their long-denied freedom.

Abisai was among the slaves who had managed to escape the clutches of their captors and flee the ill-fated slave ship. Yet, after his harrowing escape, he found himself adrift and directionless, unsure of how to find his way back home. Seeking safety and refuge, he banded together with a small group of fellow survivors, embarking on a perilous journey through the uncharted wilderness. As they ventured through unfamiliar terrain, they stumbled upon a mighty river that would come to define their quest: the Zambezi River. They hoped its winding course would guide them homeward, leading them to inland routes that promised safety. Despite their unflagging determination, their journey did not unfold as they had anticipated. Navigating through countless trials and tribulations, they ultimately reached Northern Rhodesia, known today as Zambia, falling short of their original destination but finding solace in their newfound freedom.

Abisai's arduous pursuit of liberation took an unforeseeable detour when he became infatuated with a charismatic woman he chanced upon in Zambia. Despite their disparate origins, they forged an indomitable connection, culminating in the birth of two cherubic children. Yet, despite the deep love he held for his newfound family, Abisai's yearning to return to his ancestral land of Kenya where he wqs captured burned unceasingly within him. He had originally planned to walk an astounding 2,500 kilometers through uncharted territory across Tanzania to reach Kenya, but his romantic detour in Zambia made that journey impossible. Despite this setback, Abisai did not lose hope. For the next three years, he contemplated and crafted a strategy to make his way back to the seashore, aiming to reorient himself and find a path towards his homeland Kenya. His determination never wavered, as he envisioned the day he would finally return to the land of his birth.

Nevertheless, his partner was adamant about joining him on the journey. Despite her enthusiasm, Abisai recognized the perils that lay ahead, particularly in the coastal areas where ruthless slave traders frequently abducted unsuspecting victims for the booming black-market slave trade. He could not permit his beloved to risk her life and therefore chose to undertake the hazardous journey alone. The routes would be treacherous, and the dangers only grew more menacing as he approached the coast. Inland villages were hotspots for kidnappings, where unsuspecting individuals were captured and sold, but Abisai hoped the seashore would help him recalibrate his bearings.

At the seafront, Abisai's unyielding conviction began to falter. He was lost and disoriented, a man without a country, swept away in a sea of uncertainty. Desperate for any glimmer of hope to find his way back home, Abisai took a chance on a fishing boat, fervently praying it would lead him toward the East African shoreline. However, his aspirations were dashed when he found himself in Oluwale Kosola, a coastal town in what is today known as Benin, in West Africa. Here, Abisai discovered a hidden world of treachery and deceit, as rumors circulated of the slave trade's clandestine revival. The town, with its bustling markets and shadowy alleys, was a stark reminder of the perils that still lurked. Amidst the whispers of the trade's resurgence, Abisai navigated this dangerous landscape, his hope of reaching home now interwoven with the urgent need to evade capture and survive in an environment fraught with hidden threats.

Despondent and disillusioned, Abisai felt as though his journey home was an impossible dream. Yet, his hope flickered back to life when he found refuge in a community of the Yoruba people, just a few kilometers inland. For a brief time, he felt safe and protected, embracing the warmth of this new-found sanctuary. But the cruel hand of fate soon snatched away even this fragile sense of security.

One chilly evening, as the sun dipped below the horizon and the village settled into an uneasy calm, Abisai and his companions were suddenly attacked by the neighboring Dahomian tribe. Their ferocity and skill in battle left no chance for escape. The Dahomian tribesmen descended like a storm, their warriors clad in dark, menacing garb their faces painted with fearsome designs that gleamed in the fire light. Spears and machetes glinted ominously as they swept the village with lethal precision. The night was filled with the clash of weapons and cries of despair, as Abisai once again found himself thrust into a desperate struggle for survival amidst the chaos and carnage. He felt a searing pain as he stumbled over a fallen comrade, his vision blurring with smoke and tears. The air was thick with scent of burning wood and the coppery tang of blood. He could hear the guttural commands of the Dahomian leaders, urging their warriors on with ruthless efficiency. In the midst of the melee, Abisai fought to protect himself and those around him, his muscles straining with each desperate blow. Yet, the Dahomians' ferocity was overwhelming. Warriors moved with the precision of predators, striking down anyone in their path.

The Dahomians subdued and captured over a hundred people, including Abisai, and marched them to the coast into a holding barracoon, where they were quickly stripped and shackled. This was Abisai's new reality. The Barracoon was a grim overcrowded enclosure, its air thick with despair and the stench of human suffering. As fate would have it, yet again, Abisai and his companions found themselves in the grip of another unforeseen circumstance. They were purchased by a white man who went by the name of Captain William Foster, and soon they were herded onto a ship. It was no ordinary vessel, however, but the infamous Clotilda, notorious for being the last slave ship to ever reach the shores of the continental United States.

The Clotilda's deck was a scene of utter chaos as the captives were driven aboard, their shackles clinking ominously with each step. The ship's hold was a cramped, suffocating space, filled with the terrified murmurs of those who shared Abisai's fate. The reality of their predicament pressed down on them like a physical weight, each moment a relentless reminder of their captivity. The journey ahead promised nothing but hardship and torment, yet Abisai clung to the faint hope that somehow, against all odds, he might find a way to survive and perhaps, one day, taste freedom again.

The Clotilda's sails billowed in the wind as the ship set course for the unknown, carrying with it the stolen lives and shattered dreams of Abisai and his fellow captives.

Despite the terror and uncertainty that must have gripped Abisai and his fellow captives, they could not have known the full extent of the horror that awaited them. For they were unwittingly boarding the very last ship to ever carry slaves to the Americas, and their journey would be scarred by unimaginable torment and brutality. The Clotilda was a ship of infamy, a floating prison of hopelessness that would go down in history as a chilling reminder of man's inhumanity to man.

The hold was a dark, airless chamber where the captives were packed tightly together, their bodies pressed against one another in stifling confinement. The stench of sweat, blood, and human waste permeated the air, creating an atmosphere of unbearable misery.

As the Clotilda cut through the waters, the captives endured relentless suffering. Each day brought new trials as they faced starvation, disease, and the ever-present threat of violence from the crew. The ship's deck was a place of dread, where any attempt at resistance was met with swift and brutal punishment. The Atlantic stretched out before them, an endless expanse of water that symbolized their despair. Every wave that rocked the ship seemed to echo their own turbulent emotions—fear, anger, and a flickering hope that somehow, they might survive this ordeal. Yet, the Clotilda's grim reputation ensured that their journey was one of constant dehumanization and agony.

In the face of such horror, Abisai and his companions could do little but cling to their resilience and the faintest glimmer of hope. Their passage on the Clotilda would forever be etched in the annals of history, a stark testament to the cruelty inflicted upon countless souls in the name of greed and exploitation.

Abisai and his fellow captives were now ensnared in the merciless grip of the illegal slave trade, torn from their families and homes and thrust into a nightmare of unimaginable cruelty and suffering. Their fate hung in the balance as they were transported across the treacherous waters of the Atlantic, destined for a land they could never have imagined.

As the Clotilda surged through the turbulent ocean, Abisai's heart sank under the weight of his misfortune. The full, crushing realization of his plight bore down on him: once again, he found himself at the mercy of ruthless captors, thrust into a life of misery and servitude with no hope of escape. The future seemed bleak and hopeless, a far cry from the dreams he had once harbored of returning home to his family and loved ones.

Days crawled by and the ship's hold slowly became a suffocating dungeon, filled with the pained murmurs and quiet sobs of those around him. Each day melded into the next in a haze of hunger, disease, and despair. Abisai's spirit, though resilient, was battered by the relentless cruelty and the seemingly endless journey toward an unknown and terrifying destination. His thoughts often drifted back to his homeland, the vibrant landscapes of Kenya, and the loved ones he had been torn from. Those memories became his solace, a fragile thread of hope that he clung to amidst the overwhelming darkness. Yet, as the days turned into weeks, even these memories began to fade under the relentless weight of his suffering.

The air was thick with the stench of death and despair as Abisai finally disembarked from the Clotilda. More than forty days of torture at sea had left him emaciated and broken, his spirit nearly crushed by the cruelty he had endured. As he stumbled onto the shore of Mobile Harbor on that fateful night of July 9, 1860, all he could see was a cold, gray moonlight filtering down through the bushes and onto the faintly gleaming sand.

The air was heavy with the stench of misery and decay, and Abisai knew that his future was uncertain at best. Together with his fellow captives, they were immediately forced to hide in the delta swamp, a labyrinth of murky water and dense foliage, without clothing for days as their sale was arranged. Eventually, the captives were split up and sold off to several sprawling cotton plantations of Alabama. The once cohesive group was torn apart, their bonds severed by the merciless trade. Abisai found himself toiling from sunrise to sunset under the blistering sun, the weight of his chains a constant reminder of his captivity. The days were grueling, each moment filled with backbreaking labor as he and his fellow slaves worked the fields with aching hands and weary bodies.

The crack of the overseer's whip was a cruel soundtrack to their days, its sharp report a constant threat that drove them to their physical limits. Those who faltered under the intense workload faced brutal punishment, their cries of pain echoing through the fields. Abisai's body bore the scars of his ordeal, each lash a testament to the relentless suffering imposed upon him.

Despite the overwhelming hardship, a small flame of resilience burned within Abisai. His dreams of returning home, though faint and distant, sustained him through the darkest of times. The plantation's oppressive regime sought to break their spirits, but the hope of freedom and reunion with loved ones kept Abisai and his companions clinging to whatever shreds of hope they could muster.

Despite the harshness of their circumstances, Abisai and his companions refused to be broken. They endured the backbreaking work and the constant threat of violence with a steely determination that belied their dire situation. Through it all, Abisai remained resolute in his quest for freedom. He plotted and planned, biding his time until the perfect moment to make his escape. His courage and tenacity proved an inspiration to his fellow captives, who looked up to him in the face of such overwhelming odds. As the months turned into years, Abisai continued to work tirelessly in the cotton fields, never losing sight of his ultimate goal. Though the road ahead would be long and fraught with danger, he remained steadfast in his determination to one day taste freedom once more. Every night, as he lay beneath the starry Alabama sky, Abisai whispered prayers for guidance and strength. He knew that the path to liberation would be fraught with peril, but he refused to let fear hold him back.

At long last, on June 19th, 1865, a momentous day arrived, delivering news of emancipation that spread like wildfire throughout the states, extinguishing the brutal era of slavery and slave trade outright. For Abisai and his fellow survivors, this day marked a profound turning point, a chance to reclaim their freedom and restore their dignity. They had endured indescribable horrors, stripped of their families, culture, and identity, but they had never lost hope. The news of emancipation brought a wave of emotion that surged through them like a mighty river, washing away the pain of their past.

As the shackles of slavery finally shattered, Abisai felt a flood of relief and joy. Tears streamed down his face, mingling with the sweat and dirt that had been a constant part of his existence. He looked around at his companions, their faces alight with the same mixture of disbelief and elation. Together, they had weathered the storm, and now they stood on the precipice of a new beginning. The fields that had once been their prison now seemed to transform before their eyes. The oppressive weight of the overseer's whip and the relentless sun faded into the background as they embraced their newfound freedom. Abisai's heart swelled with renewed optimism and a sense of possibility he had almost forgotten.

Though their journey had been filled with agonizing pain and hardship, they now faced the future with new faith in their spirit and a steadfast determination to carve out a better life for themselves and their families. The road ahead would not be easy, but for the first time in years, it was a road they could walk as free men and women, with their heads held high and their spirits unbroken.

Abisai gazed at the horizon, where the sun was beginning to set, casting a golden glow over the land. It felt symbolic—a powerful end to a dark chapter and the dawn of a new era. He vowed to honor the memory of those who had not survived and to build a future that would ensure their sacrifices were never forgotten. As he took his first steps into this new life, Abisai carried with him the unyielding hope and resilience that had sustained him through the darkest of times, ready to embrace the boundless possibilities of freedom.

For Abisai, it was a moment of unbridled joy and a turning point in his life. But he was still deeply scarred by the years of oppression and suffering he had endured. The legacy of slavery would continue to haunt him, and his descendants for generations to come. After slavery was abolished and Abisai and many others set free, he palpably wanted to go back to Africa but had no way or passage to travel back home to his family whom he had not seen for many years and now had little likelihood of ever seeing again in this world. Abisai's heart ached for his home in Africa, but with no means of return, he had to settle for the next best thing: a piece of land to call his own.

He approached his former owner, hoping for some sort of compensation for his years of servitude but the response he received was nothing short of cruel: an offer to purchase a portion of the very land he had toiled on for so long. Abisai felt a mixture of anger and frustration at the injustice of it all. He had labored for years on that land, working tirelessly from dawn until dusk, yet he was still denied the opportunity to claim a piece of it as his own. It was yet another bitter reminder of the cruel and arbitrary nature of the world he lived in. The sting of the former owner's words cut deep. To be asked to pay for the soil he had sweat over, bled into, and nearly died upon felt like a final, twisted mockery of his suffering. Abisai's hands, calloused and worn from years of relentless work, trembled with a mix of indignation and helplessness. The land that should have symbolized his emancipation was being dangled before him as an unattainable dream, a cruel mirage in the desert of his despair.

Despite the bitter taste of this arrangement, Abisai accepted the offer and worked tirelessly to save up enough money. He scraped together what little he had to buy two acres of land in his name. It was a small victory, but a victory nonetheless. Over time, other freed slaves joined Abisai in purchasing parcels of land, and together they formed what is today known as Africatown - a community of black individuals who refused to let their heritage be erased by the horrors of slavery. Here, they embraced their African culture, spoke their native languages, and kept their traditions alive, creating their own version of Africa right in the heart of Alabama. Though Abisai never made it back to his home continent, he found solace in this close-knit community, where he lived out the rest of his days with newfound dignity and belonging. While the physical journey back to Africa remained an impossibility, Abisai sought to keep his heritage alive in other ways. He taught his children and grandchildren the stories and traditions of his people, ensuring that the memory of their roots would not be lost. His land became a sanctuary, a place where the spirit of Africa could flourish even in a foreign land.

Abisai's legacy lived on through his children and their descendants, but with each passing generation, the details of his story became more distant and obscure. It was up to Helena, the last surviving member of Abisai's lineage, to preserve his memory and the history of the transatlantic slave trade. As Helena shared Abisai's story with her daughter Tusoli, the weight of the past was palpable. The horrors and injustices that Abisai endured were almost unimaginable, but they were a vital part of their family's history and the history of African Americans as a whole. Tusoli listened with rapt attention as her mother spoke, realizing the profound importance of passing down this knowledge to future generations. For Tusoli, the story of Abisai was not just a distant history lesson, but a personal and powerful narrative that connected her to her ancestors and their struggles.

She resolved to carry on the legacy of her family and keep Abisai's story alive, knowing that it was not just their history, but a story that belonged to all of humanity. Helena watched as Tusoli's eyes widened with horror and disbelief at the story of the slave ship. She could see the pain and anger building inside her daughter as she listened to the details of the voyage, imagining the suffering of those helpless men, women, and children. As the story continued, Helena's own emotions began to stir. She felt the weight of her ancestors' struggles and sacrifices, and the responsibility of passing down their legacy to her daughter. She knew that this tradition, passed down for generations, was not just a mere formality, but a sacred duty to keep their history alive and honor the resilience of their people. With each passing moment, the atmosphere grew thicker with a mix of sorrow, anger, and determination. Tusoli's eyes glinted with an intense fire, and Helena felt a sense of pride swelling in her chest. She knew that her daughter had the strength and passion to carry on the legacy of her ancestors, and to fight for a better world where such atrocities could never happen again.

At that moment, Helena realized that this was not just a meal to celebrate a birthday and a graduation, but a sacred ceremony to honor the past, embrace the present, and pave the way for a better future. As she enjoyed her well-prepared sumptuous meal, Tusoli was filled with astonishment, amazement, and delight as her mother Helena recounted the historic events that had unfolded in their family's past. Tusoli's heart was racing with anticipation as she asked her mother the question that had been on her mind since the beginning of the conversation.

"If the trade was illegal by then, was anyone arrested?" she inquired.

Helena took a deep breath before answering.

"The international slave trade had already been outlawed long before Abisai arrived in the Americas aboard The Clotilda, but that didn't stop some from brazenly importing slaves in defiance of the ban," she explained.

"One Alabama plantation owner made a wager that he could bring a shipload of people from Africa to the United States. And he sent Captain William Foster to buy the slaves in West Africa. To cover their tracks and hide all evidence, *The Clotilda* slave ship was set ablaze and sunk along the banks of the Mobile River. Unfortunately, to this day, no one has been held accountable for this horrific crime."

Helena gently pushed the wooden box towards her daughter, saying,

"Open it. That's 160 years of our story."

Tusoli's hands trembled as she opened the box, and the first thing she saw was a pale black and white passport photo; "Who's this, ma?" she asked, her voice barely above a whisper.

Helena's eyes glistened with tears as she replied, "That's Abisai, your forefather."

The burden of their family's history lay heavily on their hearts, a legacy of pain and injustice that could not be ignored or forgotten. Gazing at the old photograph of him, Tusoli was overcome with a profound sense of sorrow and indignation at the atrocities his forfather and countless others had endured during the dark era of the slave trade.

The depths of his suffering were beyond her comprehension, from being torn away from his family and homeland to the brutalities of life on the cotton plantations. And yet, she knew that this weight, this burden, could not be cast aside; it was a part of their family's history, a part of who they were. And so she vowed to carry it with her for the rest of her days, retelling the story to future generations, and ensuring that the memory of Abisai and his fellow survivors would never fade from history.

Hugging her mother warmly, Tusoli couldn't help but wonder why humanity could be so cruel to one another. Why did people have to suffer such indignities and atrocities at the hands of their fellow human beings? She voiced her thoughts to her mother, wondering why slavery had ever been deemed necessary when simple job opportunities and fair pay would have sufficed. Her mother sighed, unable to give a satisfactory answer. "I don't know, my darling. We can only wish that it never happened, but the truth is, it did. And it has left a deep scar on the hearts and souls of our people that will never truly heal. But what we can do is honor the memory of our ancestors by carrying their stories and legacies forward, and by standing up against any form of oppression and injustice wherever we may find it."

Tusoli nodded in agreement, feeling a newfound sense of purpose and responsibility. She may not be able to change the past, but she could help shape the future by educating others and standing up for what was right. The legacy of Abisai and his fellow slaves would live on through her and her future generations, a reminder of the resilience, strength, and courage of the human spirit in the face of unimaginable adversity. Tusoli was totally inundated by the discovery of her history. It's here that she caught this fierce pride in her color and where she truly came from. She felt a deep connection with her skin and the land where her forefathers were stolen from and their families ripped apart. Tusoli's world was forever changed by the discovery of her ancestors' history.

She checked deeper into the wooden box, feeling an overwhelming sense of pride in her heritage and connection to the land from which her forefathers were taken. It was as if she had finally found the missing piece of herself that she had been searching for. As she sifted through the preserved items and notes, her fingers brushed against a small, timeworn piece of paper. On it, in elegant, flowing script, were the words:

"One without knowledge of their history is akin to a wild tree bereft of roots."

"That was actually written by your grandma and added to the box," Helena told her.

The words resonated deeply, striking a chord within her. She placed the note over her heart with a smile, feeling a profound connection to her lineage. In that moment, she understood that the strength and resilience of her ancestors flowed through her veins, grounding her in a legacy that was as rich and enduring as the land they had come from.

Helena then pointed out a small cloth with names written on it—the names of Abisai's wives and children in Kenya and Zambia. Tusoli was awed that even with the limited education of their time, they had found a way to preserve and pass down their family history. As they talked about her forefather's life, Tusoli couldn't help but wonder if he had ever been able to return to Africa and reunite with his family. Helena's response was heartbreaking:

"No, he could not return. He never even had the chance to try. There was no passage back to their families available for him or any other slaves who were freed."

The reality of their situation hit Tusoli hard, but she knew that she would carry the stories of her ancestors with her always, honoring their memory and the sacrifices they made for future generations. She felt immense gratitude towards her mother for preserving and divulging their poignant yet captivating history. Immersing herself in this tradition instilled in her a profound sense of pride, and she now recognized with certainty that she was truly a Daughter of Africa.

Tusoli gently traced the names on the cloth, feeling a deep connection to those who came before her. The weight of their sacrifices and resilience settled within her, not as a burden, but as a source of strength. She understood that their struggles and triumphs were etched into her very being, and it was now her responsibility to ensure their legacy endured.

As she looked into her mother's eyes, she saw a reflection of the determination and hope that had carried their ancestors through the darkest of times. Tusoli vowed to honor their memory by living a life that celebrated their heritage and acknowledged the depths of their suffering and strength.

The stories Helena shared, coupled with the tangible relics of their past, wove a rich tapestry of history that Tusoli would carry with her forever. The bond she felt with her forefathers was unbreakable, a testament to the enduring spirit of those who had come before her. In that moment, she felt not only the pride of her lineage but also the profound responsibility to pass these stories to future generations, ensuring that the legacy of Abisai and his descendants would never be forgotten.

Tusoli gently closed the wooden box, watching as her mother's hand disappeared beneath the table mat; her curiosity piqued. She had always been fascinated by the old family photos that her mother kept hidden away, treasured remnants of a time long gone. As her mother's hand reemerged, Tusoli saw that she held a worn and faded picture, the edges frayed and the colors muted by age.

"Oh, there's something else. Have this too," her mother said, her voice tinged with nostalgia.

"What's that?" Tusoli asked, her eyes widening with excitement as she took another photo from her mother's outstretched hand and studied it closely. The image showed a man in a military uniform, his face set with determination, yet his eyes were kind and warm.

"Wow, I remember him very clearly, Mum. I wish he was here to celebrate my graduation with me tomorrow," Tusoli said in a sad voice, tracing the contours of her father's face with her finger.

"This was brought to me by Rudolph after the war in Afghanistan where your father died. He was my hero and the best among the marines in the time he served," Helena explained, her voice heavy with emotion.

"May he forever rest in eternal peace. He died fighting for his country. He was a hero just like Abisai. I miss him every day," Tusoli replied, her own heart swelling with sorrow.

"Did you ever tell him about our history? Did you show him this box?" Tusoli asked, her curiosity deepening.

"Yes, we opened it together right here in this house when it was still your grandma's. That was before he left for Afghanistan. You were just fourteen, Tusoli," Helena replied, her eyes misty with memories.

"Yeah, and he never returned," Tusoli said, with sadness in her voice.

"I'll go get some sleep. Get some rest too, you have a long day tomorrow. I'm proud of you, Tusoli," Helena said, the memory of her husband's death causing her poignant grief that stung her bitterly and prevented her from continuing the conversation.

"Good night, Mom. I love you," Tusoli responded, in a tender voice.

Helena gracefully slipped out of the room, leaving Tusoli to her thoughts as she sat at the dining table, still mesmerized by the photo of her father. The room was quiet, save for the faint ticking of the old clock on the wall, a soothing rhythm that seemed to echo the heartbeat of the house.

Her mind drifted into a light daydream as she reminisced about the man who had left an indelible mark on her life. She missed him dearly and wished he was still with her. Tusoli's father had been a valiant soldier, a man of great honor and integrity, whose memory she cherished dearly. She turned the photograph over, her gaze drawn towards a set of finely wrought words inscribed delicately upon the back:

A BRAVE SOLDIER

Some days, I am in pain

Some days, I have to fight the voices of those I've slain

What is so big that you can't do it for the ones you love?

What if it's the only chance to see them I have?

Every day, I wake up and go to war

To avenge what was taken by my foe

In unknown lands, the voices of your love i hear

It shields me from the raging artillery of my enemies' tear

Will I ever come back home?

Will my Tusoli remember my face?

Will you remember the night we danced?

When I return, will you still be mine?

The message of the poem was as pertinent and significant as ever to Tusoli.

"You never truly came home, Dad, and I could never forget your face. Mum is still yours. I wish you'd let her move on. She needs to." Tusoli said silently, holding the picture of her father.

After a short moment of reminiscing, Tusoli lifted the photo with trembling fingers. She felt a surge of emotion run through her body. It was a mix of sadness and joy, as memories of her hero flooded back to her. She gazed at the photo for a moment, before carefully placing it into the wooden box, as if she were adding a precious jewel to a treasure trove. When she closed the box, the weight of its history and meaning was not lost on her. This was more than just a collection of artifacts; it was a symbol of her family's legacy, a link to the past, and a source of inspiration for the future.

She sat there, the box clutched to her heart, the legacy of her ancestors and the memory of her father interwoven into her very being. In that moment, Tusoli knew she was not alone. She was a Daughter of Africa, a bearer of her family's enduring spirit.

Tusoli knew that this box held the stories of her people, and that she was now the guardian of their memory. With great reverence, she locked the box, and held it close to her chest and made her way to her bedroom. The box felt heavier, as if pulsing with the stories and memories of those who had come before her. Each grain of wood seemed imbued with the essence of their lives, their joys, their sorrows, and their resilience.

With a gentle heave, she lifted it to the top of her wardrobe, nestling it amongst a collection of her other precious belongings. She couldn't help but wonder who the next generation of Tusoli would be, and what new stories they would add to the family's collection. For now, the wooden box would rest, waiting for its next caretaker to unlock its secrets and continue the legacy of her family's history. Tusoli turned off the light, casting the room into a gentle twilight. Moonlight peeped through her window, illuminating the wooden box with a soft, ethereal glow. As she climbed into her bed, she knew that she was part of something much greater than herself, a living link in a chain of strength and endurance that stretched back through the generations and would continue far into the future.

She lay in her bed, her mind abuzz with a flurry of thoughts and emotions, her heart laden with the gravity of her family's past. Every now and then, her gaze fell upon the wooden box, comprehending that it was not simply an assemblage of antiquated photographs and trinkets, but rather a living tribute to her own identity and her place in the world.

She couldn't really dispel the sensation that she was an integral part of something far larger than herself, that the heritage and martyrdom of her forebears had been bequeathed to her, and that it was incumbent upon her to uphold that legacy, to perpetuate the tales and reminiscences for posterity. Without knowing, Tusoli drifted into slumber, the wooden box occupying a significant place in her musings, serving as a poignant emblem of her family's yesteryear, contemporaneity, and posterity.

CHAPTER 2
A NEW CHAPTER BEGINS

The air was thick with anticipation and excitement as the graduates sat in their gowns and caps, waiting for the ceremony to begin. Tusoli felt a flutter in her stomach as she took the podium. The excitement in the air was palpable. The graduates were beaming with pride and anticipation.

"Congratulations, graduates!" Tusoli began, her voice resonating with confidence and enthusiasm. "Today marks a significant milestone in your journey of exploration, discovery, and growth. It is a momentous occasion for all of us. We are presented with yet another opportunity to explore life, to gain new knowledge and experiences, albeit in a different setting. Look how far you've come, from different parts of the world, united in your pursuit of knowledge and life lessons for the betterment of humanity."

She paused, looking around the room at the beaming faces before her. "For some of you, this is just the beginning. You're already eyeing the next step in your education, eager to take on new challenges and pursue your dreams. For others, you're itching to move on, to start your careers, to tackle the world head-on. And for some of you, you're not quite sure where life will take you next. But that's okay. Life is a journey, and sometimes the destination is just a small part of it. No matter where we stand, we have a daunting task to do good for the human race, to treat each other with equality, respect, and ethical approbation, regardless of our backgrounds or beliefs or color"

Tusoli's words were met with nods of agreement and smiles of understanding.

"But wherever you go, whatever path you choose, never forget the lessons you learned here. The friendships you forged, the struggles you overcame, the knowledge you gained, these experiences are your souvenirs from this place, and they will serve you well in your future endeavors. Whatever you become, remember those that made your journey here worthwhile. Above all, let us not forget to explore the world, to travel, to go somewhere new, and to learn about other cultures. It's a never-ending journey of discovering the beauty that the world has in store for us."

She looked out at the audience, family and friends, filled with pride and continued, "As you go out into the world, always remember the values that brought you here. Strive to make a positive impact on the world around you. And never forget where you came from - your roots are what make you strong, and your past is what shapes your future. This room is packed with friends and family, all of whom are proud of you. Your dedication, perseverance, honesty, and integrity have brought you this far. Wherever you go, never forget the role they played in your life. As my grandma once said, I quote, "One without knowledge of their history is akin to a wild tree bereft of roots." end of quote. So don't forget where you came from."

"It's an honor to read this year's graduation speech. In closing, I want to leave you with a quote from the great Nelson Mandela, who once said, "Education is the most powerful weapon which you can use to change the world." Go out into the world and use that weapon to make a positive impact, to create change, and to achieve your dreams. Congratulations, Class of 2021. The world is waiting for you. Congratulations again to all of you, and may you have great success in all your future endeavors. Am Tusoli Tolewa"

The graduates erupted in applause as Tusoli concluded her speech, feeling invigorated and ready to take on the world. They knew that the journey ahead would be challenging, but they also knew that they were well-prepared, and that they had the support and guidance of those who had helped them get to this point.

After just concluding her speech Tusoli couldn't help but reflect on her own journey to this point. The long hours of studying, the late nights spent working on assignments, the moments of doubt and uncertainty. But here she was, on the cusp of a new chapter in her life, and she felt grateful for the support of her family and friends, who had encouraged her every step of the way.

Upon leaving the podium, Tusoli was enveloped by a surge of pride. She had triumphed, and now felt prepared for whatever lay ahead. Amid the applause resonating around her, she paused momentarily to take a deep breath, surveying her surroundings. It was time to venture forth into uncharted territory, to discover the wonders of the world and all its majesty, fortified by the knowledge and expertise she had gleaned during her academic journey. The world was her oyster, and she was ready to take on whatever challenges that would come her way.

Tusoli walked down the aisle of the graduation podium with confidence and pride. She took her seat next to her mother Helena, who met her with a warm and tight embrace as whispered in her ear,

"I am so proud of you. Your father would be proud too."

Tusoli felt her heart fill with joy, knowing that her hard work and dedication had paid off and had made her mother really proud. She looked around at her fellow graduates, feeling a sense of camaraderie and pride in their shared accomplishment.

The ceremony finally came to a close, and Tusoli stood up with her fellow graduates, throwing their caps into the air in celebration. When time came, they filed out of the auditorium, family and friends gathering to celebrate the momentous occasion.

Tusoli, eager to introduce her mother to someone special, turned to her and said,

"Mom, I want you to meet someone. This is Jonathan, my boyfriend."

Helena greeted Jonathan warmly, shaking his hand with a smile,

"Hello Jonathan, I finally get to meet you. My daughter has said so much about you."

Jonathan, standing tall and confident, responded with equal warmth,

"My pleasure, ma'am. I love your daughter. Her devotion to duty and natural generosity towards others has won my heart."

A look of pride and joy spread across Tusoli's face as she heard these words, glancing over at her mother who smiled back at her.

Helena added,

"Well, she is a once-in-a-lifetime kind of woman. Take that into account."

Jonathan nodded, grateful for the words,

"Thank you, ma'am."

Tusoli was thrilled to see her boyfriend and mother getting along so well. His distinguished presence and impeccable manners had won her mother's enthusiastic approval. He appeared to be a man of refined taste and an enlightened mind, a brilliant African American scholar with an abundance of oriental learning.

When the evening set in, Tusoli and her mother returned home and were joined by their neighbors for a brief joyous celebration filled with food and drinks to celebrate Tusoli's achievement. The air was filled with laughter and happiness, creating a memorable night for her.

Amidst the celebration, Mr. Rudolph caught everyone's attention by gently clinking a spoon on the side of his glass and began his speech, "Attention, everyone! Can you hear me okay? I would like to propose a toast." This caught everyone's attention, and silence fell over the gathering.

"As most of you know, Tusoli is my goddaughter, and her father and I served as marines until his untimely demise in the Afghanistan war. Today, we are here to celebrate his daughter's success as she graduates from medicine school. I am impressed by her resilience and determination to overcome all odds to come home with first-class honors, and not with a first-born baby!"

(*The crowd burst into laughter at Rudolph's sentiments as he turned to Tusoli*)

"Your father would be so proud of you Tusoli, and I am truly overjoyed. Just like your father said to young marines back in the day, I quote: "It is not so bad a world, as some would like to make it; But whether good or whether bad, depends on how you take it."

"May you have the hindsight to know where you've been, the foresight to know where you're going, and the insight to know when you're going too far. So, ladies and gentlemen, let's raise our glasses to Tusoli and wish her many years of health, happiness, love, and prosperity. Cheers!"

Helena felt immense gratitude towards Mr Rudolph and his wife Sarahlyna. They had been a constant source of support and comfort since the passing of her husband, Morris. As former army colleagues and close friends, they had remained an integral part of her life and that of her daughter. Tusoli, in particular, had developed a special bond with Mr. Rudolph as her godfather. His presence at her graduation celebration was a testament to their strong connection, and his help with the party's preparations had not gone unnoticed.

But it is Sarahlyna who Helena is especially grateful for. During the difficult and painful grieving process, she provided unwavering support, kindness, and valuable advice. Her courteous and obliging nature had been a shining light in Helena's life during a dark time, and she will forever be indebted to her.

Helena looked around at the smiling faces of family and friends enjoying the celebration, she knew that the Rudolphs were among the most important people in her life. They had been there through thick and thin, and she felt blessed to have them as part of her chosen family. After the celebration winded down, Helena, Tusoli, and the Rudolphs shared a light-hearted moment. However, Tusoli noticed that her best friend Karina, who was also Rudolph's daughter, was absent.

"Rudolph, thank you so much. We can't express our gratitude enough. You've done so much for us," Helena said with a big smile on her face.

"It's no big deal, Helena. You are family, and family is everything. And Tusoli, your speech at the institute was great. Congratulations! I wish Morris could be here to see such a milestone made by his daughter. He would be so proud of you. He always wanted to come back home. I know he is here with you, and you've made him proud," Rudolph replied.

"This is for him, and for all of you who believed in me. Honestly, I'm upset that Dad isn't here to see all of this," Tusoli admitted.

"He is proud of you, Tusoli, no matter where he is," Rudolph reassured her.

"He loved you so much," Helena added.

"I know. Thanks, Mom. Thanks, Rudolph," Tusoli said, giving both Helena and Rudolph a hug before heading inside the house.

After sharing some laughter, Helena bid farewell to Rudolph and Sarahlyna as they departed, "Goodnight"

Helena perched gracefully on the bench in her backyard, her lustrous hair fluttering in the gentle breeze as she gazed out at the serene vista before her. This day, her cherished daughter Tusoli was her companion, and her heart brimmed with pride to have her by her side. Together, they had endured countless trials and tribulations, weathered many tempests, and yet emerged triumphant. As if by design, Tusoli joined her, bearing a bottle of crimson wine in one hand and a beaming countenance on her visage. She sat herself beside her mother, deftly pouring two glasses of wine, and they began to converse with an endless flow of words, exchanging the latest tidings and occurrences from their lives and Africatown.

Helena took a sip of wine, studying her daughter with a maternal gaze, "So, tell me, that boy Jonathan, you love him? Is he serious with you?"

Tusoli's face lit up at the mention of her boyfriend. "Yes, Mom. I definitely love him. And he's way more serious than I actually thought."

Helena nodded thoughtfully, "Well, I hope it's not a bad thing that he's too serious."

Tusoli's expression turned pensive, "Mom, I just graduated. I haven't even figured anything out yet. My whole life is right here in front of me."

Helena took her daughter's hand, giving it a reassuring squeeze, "[And for some of you, you're not quite sure where life will take you next. But that's okay. Life is a journey, and sometimes the destination is just a small part of it]-remember that statement you made in your speech earlier today?"

Tusoli nodded, a small smile curving her lips, "Yes, but I'm not even sure I want to look for a job yet."

Helena smiled, proud of her daughter's independence, "Take your time, darling. And I'm right here."

Tusoli's expression turned serious, "Mom, honestly, I mean, I'm not sure I want to stay far from you. You can't be here all alone. If I have to work miles away, I'd have to go with you."

Helena's heart swelled with love for her daughter, "My love, you don't need to worry about me. I'll be fine. This is your life now. Go for it. You have to go out there and chase your dreams."

Tusoli's eyes shimmered with unshed tears, "I'm not sure, Mom. You can't be here just by yourself."

Helena reached out to stroke her daughter's cheek, "Honey, I'll be more than happy to see you excel out of here. This has been our ancestral home for more than a century, but you have to go out there and see the world baby. I just don't want you to inherit this house like I did after your father died. You know we couldn't keep up with the rent in Montgomery. I want you to do more with your life, that's why I took you to medical school."

Tusoli nodded, her gaze dropping to the ground, "Thank you, Mom. I'll figure it out."

Suddenly, she looked up, a determined gleam in her eyes, "I want to visit Dad's grave tomorrow."

Helena's heart twisted with sorrow at the mention of her late husband, "Mind if I take you?"

Tusoli shook her head. "No, Mom. I'll be fine."

After a few minutes of silence, Tusoli turned to her mother and said, "Mom, you know, I'm grateful for everything you've done for me. I know I wouldn't be here without you, and I appreciate everything you've done to help me get to where I am today."

Helena smiled at her daughter, feeling a surge of pride and love for her, "You don't have to thank me, Tusoli. You've worked hard to get to where you are, and I'm so proud of you. I know you'll do great things in this world."

Tusoli smiled back at her mother, feeling a warmth spread through her chest. She took a sip of wine, savoring the taste, and then turned her attention back to her mother, "Mom, I know you want me to chase my dreams, but I can't help but feel guilty about leaving you here alone. You've always been there for me, and I want to be there for you too."

Helena placed her hand on her daughter's shoulder, feeling the weight of her words, "Tusoli, you don't need to worry about me. I'm strong, and I'll be fine. This is your time to explore the world, to find your place in it. Don't let anything hold you back. Not even me."

Tusoli nodded, feeling a mixture of emotions. She knew her mother was right, but it was hard to leave her behind. She took another sip of wine, then looked back up at the stars, "Mom, do you ever feel like we're just specks of dust in the universe? Like our lives are so small in the grand scheme of things?"

Helena smiled, feeling a sense of wonder at her daughter's question, "Yes, I do. But I also know that every life, no matter how small, has the power to make a difference. We might be tiny specks in the universe, but we have the ability to shine bright and leave a lasting impact on the world."

Tusoli nodded, comforted by her mother's words. They sat in silence for a few minutes, lost in thought, before Helena spoke up again.

"You know, Tusoli, I never really got the chance to chase my own dreams. The bakery I wanted to open after your father died; I had to put everything on hold to take care of you. But I don't regret it. You've been my biggest dream all along, and am more than proud."

Tusoli felt a lump form in her throat at her mother's words. She knew how much her mother had sacrificed for her, and it filled her with gratitude and love, "I love you, Mom. And I promise, I'll make the most of this life you've given me."

Helena smiled at her daughter, "I love you too, Tusoli. Now come on, let's go get some rest, you've got a long journey ahead of you tomorrow."

Tusoli's heart swelled with admiration for her mother's valiance and tenacity. She lingered on the bench, gazing heavenwards at the twinkling stars, lost in contemplation. The gentle zephyr provided a respite from the sweltering day, and the soft symphony of chirping crickets wafted through the air. Absorbed in her ruminations, she savored her wine, drifting away into a reverie about her mother.

Dear Mother
Dear mother, when you first held me in your arms,
You didn't just add up to society's statistics and norms,
You let go of your own dreams and ambitions,
To guide me through life with your unwavering convictions.
Just as you carried me in your womb,
You still hear me when I'm consumed,
by troubles and worries that come my way,
You hug me close and promise to keep the bad at bay.
I admire your strength and your endless courage,
Your adventurous spirit and your love for nature,
Your words still echo in my ear,
that "without risks, there are no rewards to be reaped, my dear".
You are a woman of indomitable spirit,
Noble, generous, and always so resolute,
You have taught me wisdom and discipline,
And your love and care, for me, is absolute.
You have been a friend, a mentor, and a guide,
And though I've grown, I'll always be the child,
for whom you sacrificed, and wore yourself out,
To give me a life that's free of any doubt.
You are my exquisite jewel, my shining light,
Whose beauty and grace are simply divine,
And the love that we share, will never be lost,
Whether I'm at home, or far away on the coast.
Oh dear mother, you mean the world to me,
And in your embrace, I'll always find the key,
To a life that's full of love, hope, and grace,
With you by my side, in every single place.

CHAPTER 3
THE GRAVE

Tusoli woke up to the sound of her phone ringing. It was Jonathan.

"Good morning, babe," she answered, her voice still heavy with sleep.

"Morning! You're up early. What's on the agenda today?" Jonathan asked.

"I'm visiting Dad's grave today. I haven't been back since the funeral," Tusoli replied softly.

"Do you want some company?" Jonathan offered.

"I think I need to do this alone," she said, her voice tinged with resolve.

"Are you sure? I can be there for you," Jonathan insisted, concern evident in his tone.

"I'm okay, honey. I just need some time by myself. How was your night? We didn't get to talk much after the graduation. It was pretty hectic here with all the neighbors visiting," Tusoli said, steering the conversation to lighter ground.

"Yeah, sorry about that. We had a party too, and it ran late," Jonathan explained.

"A party? With your college buddies?" she asked, curiosity piqued.

"Yeah, and my cousins. It was a good time," Jonathan replied.

"I hope you had fun," Tusoli said, a hint of a smile in her voice.

"It would've been more fun if you were there," he admitted, a note of longing creeping in.

"Well, I wasn't exactly invited, was I? Plus, we had our own little celebration at home," Tusoli responded.

"Never mind that. What's important is that we made it through college, and I can't wait to see what the future holds for us," Jonathan said, trying to lift her spirits.

"Yeah, let's see where life takes us," she replied thoughtfully.

"Hey, can I ask you something?" Jonathan said, hesitating for a moment.

"Of course. What is it?" Tusoli replied.

"Can we move in together?" he asked, hope in his voice.

"Don't you think it's a bit soon? We've just graduated. We need to figure things out first," Tusoli responded, taken aback by his sudden proposal.

"I know, but I love you. And my dad's already lined up a job for me at a private medical facility. We'll be fine," Jonathan reassured her.

"That's great news about the job. I love you too, but let me think about it, okay?" she said, considering the idea.

"Sure, take your time," Jonathan said, understanding.

"I've got to go now. I'll talk to you later. I love you," Tusoli said, ending the conversation.

"I love you too. Bye, and take care," Jonathan replied.

Helena called out from the kitchen, "Baby, breakfast is ready. Come on now."

Tusoli headed to the dining table, where her mother had prepared a spread of coffee, eggs, and a variety of fruits. "Thanks, Mum," she said, giving her a morning kiss on the cheek.

After they finished eating, Tusoli excused herself. "Mom, I'll get ready to leave in a few."

"Sure thing. I've packed some extra fruits for you, and Rudolph brought these flowers," Helena replied.

"Told him I was going, huh?" Tusoli asked with a smile.

"Yes, he came by this morning and thought it would be a good idea to change the flat tire on my car so you can use it," Helena said.

"I was planning on taking the bus," Tusoli said thoughtfully.

"Take my car so you can come back early," Helena suggested.

Tusoli considered it and responded, "You know Grandpa won't let me come back just like that, especially since we haven't visited him since Dad's burial. He's always asking me to visit. I think I'll spend a day or two there, and you need your car for work tomorrow."

Helena smiled warmly, "Well, he'll be surprised at how much you've grown. You were only fourteen when we buried your father."

"I'll get a shower, Mum," Tusoli said, heading upstairs.

Tusoli departed for Montgomery, the capital city of Alabama, where she had spent most of her childhood with her father. Upon arriving in Montgomery, a three-hour journey from Africatown, a wave of nostalgia swept over her, and she felt as though she was reliving her cherished childhood memories. She wandered about the city, taking leisurely strolls down the familiar streets, before continuing to her Grandpa's place. After taking in the sights and sounds of Montgomery, she pressed on to Auburn, the quaint town where her grandfather's vast estate was located. The sprawling farmland, nestled amidst rolling hills and verdant pastures, was a sight to behold.

Upon reaching her grandfather's expansive farm, Tusoli was welcomed with open arms by the elderly patriarch, who was positively elated by her unexpected arrival. Amidst the warm embrace of family, her grandfather regaled her with tales from her childhood, recounting fond memories of when she would visit for extended stays with Morris, her doting father. As she listened intently to his anecdotes, Tusoli felt nostalgia wash over her, transporting her back in time to a simpler era. Despite the passage of a dozen years since she last saw him, her grandfather appeared almost unchanged, a testament to his resilient nature.

Over a steaming cup of coffee, the two spent hours catching up, reminiscing about old times and sharing stories of their respective journeys since they last saw each other. In the midst of their conversation, Tusoli also had the pleasure of meeting her cousins, who had traveled all the way from New York to be with family. The reunion was a joyous occasion, marked by laughter and merriment as the family bonded over shared experiences and treasured memories. As the sun dipped below the horizon, casting a golden glow across the landscape, Tusoli retrieved the bouquet of flowers she had brought along and made her way towards the edge of her grandfather's sprawling farm.

Accompanied by the old man, she walked towards her father's final resting place, a serene and solemn spot overlooking the idyllic countryside. They stood in quiet contemplation before the grave for a moment, then her grandfather spoke reverently about his youngest child, Tusoli's father; "Morris had served his country with distinction, dedicating himself to the noble cause of defending his homeland until his very last breath."

Tusoli listened intently to her grandfather's words as she placed the bouquet of flowers she had brought onto her father's grave, a small token of her love and affection for the man who had left a lasting impact on her life. She stood there for a few moments, lost in thought, before turning to her grandfather with tears in her eyes, "Thank you for sharing that with me, grandfather. I never knew the extent of my father's service to our country. I miss him so much," Tusoli said, her voice choking with emotion.

Her grandfather placed a comforting hand on her shoulder, his own eyes glistening with unshed tears, "Your father was a brave and honorable man, my dear. He would be proud of the woman you've become," he said, his voice full of love and pride.

Tusoli then asked, "How exactly did my father die in Afghanistan? Now that I'm older, you can tell me."

"He was on a mission to rescue his trapped crew in Afghanistan, and he and his team of Marines ran into an explosive that destroyed their vehicle. His friend Rudolph was the only survivor," her grandfather answered.

Tusoli expressed, "I thought I'd see him again."

"I know your father. He would have done anything to come home to his family. He loved you so much. Why don't I leave you now? You need a moment with him," her grandfather replied before giving her space to reflect at the grave site.

As the sun dipped further toward the horizon, Tusoli stood in front of her father's grave, looking at the headstone with his name as the inscription:

MORRIS ANDERSON PUTH
2 MEDALS OF HONOR
6 RED 2 DIV
US MARINE CORPS
AFGHAN WAR
NOV 10 1968
NOV 10 2007
PURPLE HEART
"I DIE A TRUE SOLDIER"

Tusoli sat down at her father's grave, placing a hand on the cold stone as she spoke softly to him, her voice tinged with sadness and longing.

"Dad, there is so much I wish I could share with you. I graduated from college, just like you always wanted, and I'm starting to make my way in the world. But it's not the same without you here to see me shine, to guide me and mentor me. Your absence still weighs heavily on my heart."

Tusoli paused for a moment, her eyes misty with tears, before continuing. "I found the poem you wrote for Mom, tucked away in the back of one of your photos. She's still yours, even after all these years. And you made a wish that I would never forget your face. I promise you, I never have and never will. Your memory is forever etched in my heart."

Tusoli looked out across the peaceful countryside, her thoughts drifting back to happier times. "Do you remember the park, Dad? Those were some of the happiest moments of my life. I miss you so much, and everything about you.

After you passed away, we had to leave the city and move in with Grandma in Africatown. It was tough, and I had to change schools, but Mom and I managed."

Tusoli's gaze fell on the beautiful Roses, "Mom told me about our family history, and how we came to be. She said you opened the box with her at Grandma's. I wish you were here to tell me more about it, about our ancestors, and how it felt. But I know you're watching over me, Dad. And I'll always love you, and keep your memory alive."

"Lately, I've been feeling an urge to visit Africa. I don't know why, but there's a strong pull that I can't ignore. I wish I could talk to you about it and get your thoughts on the matter."

"I also wanted to share some news with you about my boyfriend, Jonathan. He's an exceptional gentleman, and I believe he would have earned your respect had you met him. He's been urging me to cohabitate with him, but my heart is indecisive, uncertain if such a step would be wise. Your absence gnaws at me, and I yearn for your guidance. As much as this proposal beckons, I'm also exploring career prospects, but I worry about being away from Mom for too long. She needs me, and I don't want to leave her all alone. The passing of time since your departure has been a struggle for her, and I am apprehensive about being absent when she most needs me. Perhaps a new person in her life would alleviate her distress? Can she start dating again? What do you think, dear father?"

"I express my deepest gratitude for the memories that we shared. Although our time together was tragically brief, the moments we spent together will forever hold a precious place in my heart. While I am aware that you are no longer with us in the physical realm, I wholeheartedly believe that your spirit continues to watch over and guide us."

"Happy birthday in heaven, Dad. You are forever missed and loved." Tusoli concluded.

As the sun finally descended below the horizon, welcoming the dark of the night, Tusoli approached the house where her grandfather sat outside, her steps deliberate and calm.

"I'm sure he heard you," he remarked as she approached.

Tusoli nodded, "I can feel it in my heart."

Her grandfather gestured for her to come inside. "Let's catch up. Tell me about your mother. Is she still unable to visit? We have alot to solve. She loved my son so much. I owe her a lot. And you haven't seen your cousins since the funeral."

Tusoli spent the weekend with her grandfather, uncle, and cousins, and it was a deeply satisfying time. The reunion was marked by an abundance of gaiety and laughter, as the family relished in their shared experiences and cherished memories.

CHAPTER 4
THE SHIP WRECK

My Sunshine
You are my ray of sunshine
Sweet like aged fine wine
You are my Polaris in my darkest hours
Am your garden of beautiful flowers
In a single flashing, throbbing moment
I fell deeply in love with you
You are my dream come true
I will not expect more than you can give
I have no intention of loving you by half
Because you are my perfect reflection
Whatever our souls are made of,
Yours and mine are the same.
You can doubt science,
You can doubt the moon doesn't have it's own fire,
You can doubt the sky is blue
But Just don't doubt I love you.
Because you are my Sunshine

"How was the trip, baby girl? Jonathan left you flowers and a note," Helena said, surprised by his gesture on a Monday morning when he should have been working.

Tusoli was equally surprised. "On a Monday morning? I thought he was working." She was thrilled, though, to find the flowers and a poem Jonathan had left. Reading it, she said, "He's calling me his Sunshine."

Helena couldn't help but smile. "It sounds like he really cares about you."

"Yeah, he does," Tusoli agreed. Then, she hesitantly revealed, "Jonathan asked me to move in with him."

Helena listened attentively and then cautioned, "Have you thought about what it would mean for your independence and your relationship? Moving in with someone is a big step, and you want to make sure it's what you really want."

Tusoli nodded, appreciating her mother's wisdom. "I know, Mom. I need to think it through."

"I'm still trying to figure things out myself," Tusoli admitted. "But I know I want to focus on my career for a while and see where that takes me."

Helena nodded in agreement. "That's a good plan," she said. "It's important to have your own goals and aspirations. Just make sure you're on the same page with Jonathan, so you both know what you want for your relationship. Take your time with making any big decisions. Moving in together is a big step, so make sure you're ready for it."

Tusoli appreciated her mother's advice. "I will, Mom. Thanks for the guidance," she said. "Grandpa said hello and wanted me to tell you to visit. Uncle Tim also passed his regards."

Helena's expression softened. "You know, ever since your father passed away, I haven't found the strength to visit his grave," she confessed. "And with the rest of his side of the family not on good terms with us at the time, I chose not to go. But now look how time has flown by. How about we make arrangements and go there together sometime?"

Tusoli's heart warmed at the suggestion. "I'd like that, Mom. It would be good for both of us. Grandpa will be delighted to see you, I know"

"I know, baby. So, did you talk to your Dad? What did you tell him?" Helena's eyes widened with curiosity as she leaned forward in her seat.

Tusoli shifted in her chair, a wistful look on her face. "Actually, a lot of things," she replied. "I told him I miss him and I hoped he'd be there at my graduation. I told him about Jonathan, and also about you."

Helena's interest was piqued. "What did you tell him about me?" she asked, leaning in even closer.

Tusoli took a deep breath, her eyes sparkling mischievously. "That you should see someone," she said. "Come on, Mom, go out on a date. You're not too old for dates."

Helena let out a laugh, a rare sound that filled the room with joy. "Maybe you're right," she said, her eyes twinkling with newfound hope. "Perhaps it's time to start living again. But I am happy, as long as you are doing well. That's all that matters to me."

Tusoli added, "I just want you to be happy, Mom, with a man, and Dad is okay with you moving on."

Helena laughed again. "Well, I appreciate your concern, baby girl. But right now, my focus is on making sure you are taken care of. Maybe one day, when things settle down, I'll consider it. What else did you tell him?"

Tusoli's eyes lit up with excitement as she shared her desire to travel to Africa. Helena couldn't help but burst out laughing at the unexpected declaration.

"Seriously? Africa? And you really mean it?" Helena asked, still chuckling.

Tusoli's expression turned serious. "Yes, Mom. I feel this connection I can't explain since you gave me that box. I just want to see what this place looks like. I want to visit the caves in Shimoni, maybe travel to Zambia, Benin, I don't know. I want to see where Abisai came from and stand right where he was taken onto The Clotilda."

Helena's laughter faded into a contemplative smile. "That sounds like an incredible journey, Tusoli. If it's something you truly want, I support you. It's important to connect with our roots."

Helena couldn't deny the determination in her daughter's voice. "I saw your eyes that day you opened that box, the urge in your spirit to know more. And I know my Tusoli—when she wants something, she very often gets it, against all odds," she said, nodding in admiration. "But I will tell you that there isn't much out there. All I told you is all there is to know. You could go to the slave museum right here in Alabama. I don't even know where Africa is."

Tusoli's face fell at the suggestion. "There's a museum? You never told me about it. I could check it out with Jonathan this week," she said, already thinking of ways to satisfy her hunger for more knowledge on slavery.

Helena smiled gently, seeing the eagerness in her daughter's eyes. "Yes, there's a museum. It might not be Africa, but it's a start. It can give you more context about what our ancestors went through. And who knows? It might provide some answers you've been looking for."

Tusoli's expression brightened. "Thanks, Mom. I'll talk to Jonathan about it. It's a step closer to understanding our history."

Helena reached out and took her daughter's hand. "I'm proud of you, Tusoli. Your desire to learn about our past is important. Just remember, no matter where you go or what you find, you're carrying the legacy of your ancestors with you. And that, my dear, is a powerful thing."

Tusoli squeezed her mother's hand, feeling a deep sense of connection and purpose. "I will, Mom. Thank you for everything. I'll make sure our story is never forgotten."

Helena added to her daughter's curiosity, "You can explore several museums and landmarks that offer a glimpse into our community's history and culture. One must-visit museum is the Africatown Welcome Center & Museum, dedicated to preserving the history and culture of Africatown and its people. Another interesting place is the Mobile County Training School, a historic school built in 1924 to provide education to African American children in the area. Today, it serves as a museum where you can learn about the struggles and achievements of black students during segregation."

She continued, "Lastly, don't miss the Plateau Cemetery, the final resting place of many of the original founders of Africatown, including Abisai. It's a somber yet powerful reminder of the sacrifices and contributions of those who came before us."

THE LAST SHIP WRECK

It's a beautiful Sunday morning, the kind that seems to carry a promise of warmth and tranquility. The sun's golden rays filter through the sheer curtains, casting soft, dancing patterns on the floor. Birds chirp merrily outside, adding a cheerful soundtrack to the start of the day.

In her bedroom, Helena stands before her full-length mirror, carefully selecting her sunday best. She chooses a vibrant, floral dress that flatters her figure and exudes a sense of grace. The fabric feels smooth under her fingertips as she smooths out any wrinkles, ensuring every detail is perfect. A gentle hum escapes her lips, a familiar hymn that she has sung countless times every other Sunday morning.

She reaches for her favorite hat, a wide-brimmed creation adorned with delicate flowers and ribbons that complement her dress. Placing it on her head, she adjusts it slightly, making sure it sits just right. Helena glances in the mirror, a satisfied smile spreading across her face. Her eyes sparkle with confidence and a readiness to embrace the day's blessings.

Turning to her daughter, Tusoli, who is busy with her own preparations, Helena asks with a hopeful smile, "Are we going to church, dear? It's always such a joyous experience to worship together with the community."

Tusoli paused, a glint in her eye. "Actually, Mom," she replied, "I'm planning to go on a hike with Karina and other college friends down the plateau in Mobile Bay. We want to check out *The Clotilda* discovery site."

Helena's eyes widened with surprise, "Clotilda?" she repeated, her mind racing. "The last slave ship of 1860? But I thought it was already ruled out that it wasn't *The Clotilda* that was discovered."

Tusoli nodded, a smile playing at the corners of her lips. "Actually, the Alabama Historical Commission verified the wreckage as *The Clotilda*" she said, excitement rising in her voice. "It's an opportunity to witness history and honor those who suffered through the horrors of slavery"

Helena took a moment to process this, her expression softening with understanding. "The Clotilda, the last-known slave ship to arrive in the United States, lost to the annals of history for over a century, finally found," she mused, her voice tinged with awe. "I can see why you'd want to go. Standing in the same spot where enslaved Africans once stood must be powerful."

Tusoli's eyes sparkled, "Exactly, Mom. The thought of being there, where so many suffered and endured, it sends shivers down my spine. It's not just about witnessing history; it's about honoring their legacy."

The doorbell chimed, and Tusoli hurried to answer it. "I'll get that," she called out.

"Good morning, Mrs. Rudolph," Tusoli greeted her guest with a smile. "Come in, please. I thought it was Karina. Where is she?"

"Karina? She told me you guys have a hike to do. She's already left. Where's Helena?" Mrs. Rudolph asked back, looking slightly frazzled. "We should be going for the church service. We're already late."

Helena appeared at the sound of her name. "Good morning, Sarahlyna. Let's get going," she said, grabbing her purse and heading toward the door. Turning to her daughter, she added, "See you later, sweetheart."

Tusoli hugged her mother goodbye. "See you later," she said as Helena and Mrs. Rudolph headed out the door to make it to church on time.

Tusoli anxiously called Karina's phone, but there was no answer. Frustrated, she dialed their friend Pete, hoping for some answers.

"Hey, where are you and Karina? We're already at the meeting point," Pete exclaimed even before Tusoli could say a word.

Tusoli's voice was strained. "I'm on my way. Karina isn't there yet? She was supposed to pick me. I'll be there soon."

After the call ended, Tusoli quickly made her way to the garage, hopped on her bike, and pedaled to Karina's house. Unfortunately, Karina had already left without her, so Tusoli rushed to the group's designated meeting spot just a few yards away. But upon arriving, Karina was nowhere to be found.

Pete frantically asked, "Where's Karina? She's not picking up her phone."

Tusoli called Karina again, but there was no answer.

Rachel chimed in, "Maybe she went to church. You know her father is always on her case about attending."

Tusoli shook her head, "No, Rudolph knows how important this is to us. Karina knows the way. She'll find us there. Let's go guys"

Rachel agreed, "Let's not wait any longer. We should head to the site."

Tusoli, Rachel, Pete, and their four other friends hopped on their bicycles and set off towards The Clotilda's discovery site.

The Clotilda, the last known slave ship to bring Africans to the United States, was finally within their reach. The wreckage and legacy of the ship lay just north of downtown Africatown, in the muddy banks of the Mobile River off the Atlantic. As they cycled towards the bay, the fading sun cast a warm glow over the Mobile river, and the breeze carried the smell of saltwater and marsh. Tusoli couldn't help but feel a sense of calm wash over her, even in the midst of her anxiety.

As they arrived at the desolate site, a deep feeling of reverence washed over her like a tidal wave. The air crackled with an energy that whispered tales of bygone eras, and Tusoli stood amidst the remnants of time, feeling as though she were a mere echo in a symphony of suffering and resilience.

Gazing upon the protruding skeletal remains of The Clotilda, Tusoli felt as though she stood at the crossroads of eternity, where the echoes of the past reverberated through the very fabric of the present. It was as if the spirits of those long departed danced in the shadows, their whispers carrying the weight of centuries-old sorrows and untold stories.

Each rusted fragment of the shipwreck spoke volumes, a silent testimony to the inhumanity that once stained these hallowed grounds. Tusoli had immersed herself in the labyrinthine corridors of history, unearthing the forgotten truths of slavery's darkest chapters and the enigmatic tale of The Clotilda.

As she stood before the wreckage, Tusoli was consumed by a maelstrom of emotions, each one a poignant chord in the symphony of her soul. There was awe in the face of such resilience, horror at the atrocities committed, and a profound sadness for the lives forever scarred by the chains of bondage.

Beside her stood her companions, their eyes alight with a shared understanding of the weight of the moment. Together, they bore witness to the haunting silhouette of a ship that had carried dreams and nightmares across the vast expanse of the Atlantic.

In that fleeting moment, Tusoli dared to dream of a future where The Clotilda would rise from its muddy grave, a phoenix reborn from the ashes of history. She envisioned a sanctuary where the stories of those who had suffered would be etched into the annals of memory, a testament to the resilience of the human spirit in the face of unspeakable adversity.

With a silent vow etched upon her heart, Tusoli pledged to honor the legacy of those who had come before, to ensure that their voices echoed through the corridors of time for generations to come. For in the depths of that sacred ground, amidst the wreckage of a forgotten past, she found not only despair but also the flicker of hope that illuminated the path toward a brighter tomorrow.

She imagined a museum where visitors could walk through exhibits and learn about the lives of the people who were brought to America on this ship, and the struggles they faced in their new lives as slaves. She also hoped that this museum would serve as a reminder of the dark parts of American history, and a call to action to continue the fight for equality and justice for all.

"I wish Karina and Jonathan were here too," Tusoli posed to her friends while they took the photos."

After they wrapped up their work in Mobile Bay and prepared to depart, Tusoli reached for her phone and dialed Jonathan's number. But the call went unanswered and was promptly directed to voicemail. Frustrated by her unsuccessful attempt to reach him, Tusoli decided to contact her best friend Karina, only to encounter the same outcome - her friend did not pick up. The mounting sense of annoyance within her began to simmer, as they all mounted their bikes and began the journey back along the well-trodden sandy path of the Mobile River. While they rode, the fiery sun began its descent, casting a resplendent glow over the stunning beauty of Africatown.

At the converging point, they stopped and gathered around, chatting and laughing about their day, taking in the beauty of the setting sun. The echoes of history surrounded them.

"This was a great idea, Tusoli. We should do this more often." Rachael spoke

Pete chimed in, "Definitely. It's amazing how much of our history is right here in our own backyard."

Tusoli nodded in agreement, "Yeah, and it's so important to understand and learn from that history and to never forget."

They eventually said their goodbyes and started to go their separate ways. Tusoli asked Pete if he could ride with her. The frustration in her voice was palpable as she tried to reach Jonathan and Karina with no success.

"Why aren't they picking up? What could be going on?" Tusoli asked Pete, frustration evident in her voice.

"Perhaps they're simply occupied or dealing with poor reception. Try not to worry too much," Pete replied in an attempt to reassure her.

"I can't help but worry," Tusoli persisted. "Something doesn't feel right. Where could they be? This is really strange."

"Jonathan could be busy with work. Let's not jump to conclusions just yet," Pete suggested.

"But I've been trying to reach him all day and he's not answering. Could he really be working on a Sunday? It's just that it's not like Jonathan to not answer his phone, and Karina usually lets us know if she's going to be unavailable." Tusoli fretted.

"Let's give it a little more time. Maybe he'll call back or we'll hear from Karina as well," Pete offered, hoping to quell Tusoli's growing anxiety.

Tusoli reluctantly agreed, but her worry wouldn't dissipate. She couldn't shake the feeling that something was amiss.

In recent days she had noticed the change in the man she had so gradually grown to love, and her heart was beating in wild tumult. She stood, in her young purity, at one end of the chain for years, maybe an ascetic who dreamed of a happily ever after. But Jonathan; did he really stand at the other?

Tusoli bid farewell to her friend, Pete, but her mind was ablaze with questions as she pedaled her bike along the beaten tarmac towards her home. The perplexing situation with Jonathan couldn't leave her thoughts, and she was plagued by a persistent unease. What could be happening with him? Why would he deceive her? These and other queries raced through her mind, leaving her feeling adrift in a sea of uncertainty. However, a sense of satisfaction was lingering within her heart. The experience of discovering *The Clotilda* wreck, an essential piece of history, had left her feeling fulfilled. Despite the underlying concerns regarding Jonathan, she attempted to push these thoughts to the back of her mind and soak in the beauty of the sunset and the caress of the cool breeze against her skin. With a clear head, she pulled up into her driveway and parked her bicycle in the garage before making her way to Karina's house.

"Hi Mrs. Rudolph, how are you? Is Karina in?" Tusoli inquired.

"Yes, she's in her room, dear," Sarahlyna replied, flanging the door wide.

Tusoli rushed upstairs and entered Karina's room, confronting her about their missed Clotilda hike and her lack of communication.

"What's wrong with you, Karina? We were supposed to go on the Clotilda hike together, and you didn't show up or return my calls," Tusoli demanded.

"Hey, Tusoli, I thought you should knock," Karina replied.

"Since when did I knock on your door, Karina? What's going on with you?" Tusoli questioned, her concern deepening.

"Can I just not talk about it today?" Karina requested, her voice strained.

"No, you have to talk to me, Karina. Right now," Tusoli insisted, her frustration growing.

"My head is spinning, Tusoli. I need to rest," Karina pleaded, looking exhausted.

"Fine!" Tusoli stormed out of Karina's room and left the house, running into Rudolph just as he was arriving.

"Tusoli, wait up. Is everything okay?" Rudolph asked, noticing her distress.

"I'm alright, Mr. Rudolph. Just a little frustrated with Karina," Tusoli replied, trying to keep her emotions in check.

"I understand. I know she's been going through a tough time lately," Rudolph said sympathetically.

"What's been going on with her?" Tusoli asked, her worry evident.

"I don't want to speak out of turn, but I know she's been dealing with some personal issues. I'll head up and talk to her. I'm sure she'll tell you when she's ready," Rudolph assured her.

"I just wish she would talk to me. We've been friends for so long, all our childhood," Tusoli said, her voice softening with concern.

"I know, and she values your friendship too. Just give her some space and let her come to you when she's ready," Rudolph advised, giving her a reassuring smile.

As Rudolph walked into Karina's room, he found her lying on the bed with her face buried in the pillow. "Hey dear, what's going on? Is everything alright?" he asked gently.

Karina looked up at her father, tears streaming down her face. "Dad, I don't know what's happening to me. I feel so lost and confused."

Rudolph sat down on the edge of the bed and put his arm around her. "It's okay, Karina. You can talk to me about anything. What's been bothering you?"

Karina took a deep breath and began to open up. "I've been struggling with anxiety and depression. I feel so overwhelmed and disconnected from everyone. I can't sleep, I can't focus on my schoolwork. Everything just feels so hard."

Rudolph listened patiently, offering comfort and reassurance. "It's alright, Karina. I'm here for you. You're not alone in this. We can get through it together."

"I just... I didn't want to worry you or anyone else," Karina said, her voice breaking.

"I love you, Karina, and your well-being is the most important thing to me," Rudolph said, hugging her tightly. "We'll find a way to help you feel better. You're stronger than you think."

Karina eventually calmed down, feeling a sense of relief from sharing her burden. "Thanks, Dad. I really needed to hear that."

"Anytime, sweetheart. Now rest up, and we'll take it one step at a time," Rudolph said, giving her a reassuring smile before leaving her to rest.

Tusoli's mind was racing with thoughts as she made her way back to her house, consumed with frustration and anger towards Karina. She couldn't understand why her best friend wouldn't open up to her, and it was worrying her deeply to think of what could be happening in Karina's life. Upon entering her home, she made a decision to call Jonathan again, hoping that he would answer this time. The phone rang incessantly, but there was no response. Tusoli left a message, her tone laced with concern, requesting Jonathan to call her back at his earliest convenience. The gnawing sense of worry that she felt for Karina was now expanding to include Jonathan as well.

Tusoli decided to distract herself from everything by cooking dinner, hoping that the act of chopping vegetables and stirring pots would help her calm down. She put on some music and lost herself in the task, feeling a little better as the savory smells of cooking food filled her kitchen. She set the table for two, and when her mom arrived, they had dinner together before Tusoli headed straight to bed; but sleep eluded her. She tossed and turned, unable to shake off the nagging worry that had taken root in her mind. She kept reaching for her phone, hoping to see a missed call or message from Jonathan, but there was nothing. Should she call him again or wait until the morning? She debated with herself for a while before finally deciding to give him one more try. This time, to her relief, he answered the phone, but she could barely hear him over the din of people in the background. Tusoli's anger dissipated and she breathed a sigh of relief hearing Jonathan's voice. She hoped he wouldn't lie to her and tried to trust him.

"Hey, Jonathan, where have you been all day? I've been trying to call you," Tusoli said with a hint of frustration in her tone.

"I'm sorry, I couldn't talk earlier. I've been working all day, and it's been hectic here at the hospital. We had an emergency, and I've been on my feet since morning. I couldn't even take a break," Jonathan replied, explaining the situation.

Tusoli's mind eased at the sound of his voice, and she felt grateful for his explanation.

"Oh, I'm sorry. I didn't know. I was worried about you, and I thought something had happened," Tusoli said, apologetically.

"No worries. I should have called you earlier, but I've been so busy. Is everything okay with you?" Jonathan asked, showing concern.

"Yes, everything is fine. We went to *The Clotilda* discovery site today, and I tried to call you, but you were unreachable," Tusoli informed him.

"Oh, I'm sorry about that love. At some point I turned off my phone to focus on work, and I haven't checked it since," Jonathan said, acknowledging his mistake.

"It's okay. I just wanted to make sure you were okay. I'll let you get back to work now. Take care," Tusoli replied, understanding his busy schedule.

"You too, Tusoli. I will call you when I get home. I love you," Jonathan said, ending the conversation with a sweet gesture.

"I love you too," Tusoli replied, feeling content that everything was okay between them. She felt relieved after the call.

Though she was still a little hurt that Jonathan didn't tell her earlier that he would be working, she realized that she had jumped to conclusions without giving him the benefit of the doubt. She apologized to him later that night and explained how she had felt. They made up and promised to communicate better in the future.

CHAPTER 5
THE SURPRISE

Jonathan called Tusoli, but she answered the phone with a hint of anger in her voice. Their relationship had been facing a few ups and downs in recent months.

"Hello, my love," Jonathan spoke gently.

Tusoli didn't respond immediately, leaving a palpable silence on the line.

Jonathan tried to break the tension. "Let's meet at our favorite spot at 6 pm. I'll be waiting for you."

Tusoli responded with a curt, "Alright," before hanging up.

After unsuccessfully attempting to call Karina, Tusoli became concerned. She had never seen her friend act so distant for weeks now. Unable to fathom what could be causing this change in behavior, she decided to give Karina some space to work through her issues and recover. Still worried, Tusoli sent a text to Karina offering her support.

"Hey best friend, I'm here for you whenever you want to talk. You mean the world to me, and I'm less than a mile away if you need me. Take care."

Tusoli busied herself with household chores, tidying up the living room and kitchen, and making sure everything was in order. Despite her earlier conversation with Jonathan, she couldn't shake off the feeling of unease that had been bothering her all day. As she got ready for her evening date with him, Tusoli couldn't help but wonder what had been going on with him lately. She hoped that he would have some good explanations for his recent strange behavior. She took a long shower allowing the hot water to soothe her frayed nerves and calm her racing thoughts. After her shower, she took extra time selecting her outfit for the evening, opting for something that would flatter her figure and showcase her natural beauty, making sure to look her best. Tusoli knew that Jonathan appreciated when she put effort into her appearance, and she wanted to make a good impression tonight. She donned a flattering cone dress that accentuated her curves, and paired it with beige sneakers, all set for her date with Jonathan.

Just before 6pm, she stepped out into the golden-hued, fading sunset of Africatown and arrived at Louis Coffee Bar, their go-to spot for dates, which seemed like the perfect choice once again. Tusoli pushed open the glass door to enter the nicely orchestrated café feeling a mix of excitement and anticipation. As she stepped inside, she was hit with the sweet aroma of freshly brewed coffee and the sound of a beautifully articulated violin recital. To her surprise, it was Jonathan playing the instrument with such precision and skill that she was left utterly speechless. She took her seat, her gaze fixed on Jonathan as he played, each note resonating deeply within her. In front of her, a small placard displayed her name, adding a personal touch to the evening. Tusoli's heart swelled with joy, yet a touch of confusion lingered. Why this grand gesture now, after the recent turbulence in their relationship? Still, she couldn't help but be captivated by the effort and thoughtfulness Jonathan had put into this moment.

My crown princess
To that very noble lady that just popped in,
The crown Princess,
Who's won the world's unsparing approval,
No one could have been more entirely acceptable to my father.
You make my mind spin on its imaginary axis,
Without you I become a little delirious,
My heart's systole and diastole.
With you my life becomes more rapturous.
Our love is a beautiful Platonic perfection,
Yet I know I'll wait until you'll be ready,
To feel the warmth of your skin's affection,
You are my panacea, oh my pretty remedy.
You are the reason every day am strong,
Help me today to write every wrong,
In my heart it's where you belong,
I'll be loyal and faithful to you,

My one and only love.

While Jonathan played the violin, Tusoli couldn't help but feel completely enraptured by the beauty of the recital. His fingers moved expertly over the strings, eliciting a range of emotions with every note. His voice, too, was a perfect accompaniment, adding a layer of expressiveness and power to the already stunning performance. She was completely taken by the sound, feeling as though she was being transported to another world altogether. In that moment, everything else faded away, and all that mattered was the enchanting music filling the air around them.

Tusoli was in awe of Jonathan's astute performance, it was really well curated and executed. How he turned the really small café into a poetry theater melted her heart. The few people who were present gave him a round of applause for a surprise proficiently executed. The rhythmical composition gave Tusoli an exciting pleasure.

He played the prelude with such amazing poetry, that charming melody, so well suited to the words that it left Tusoli completely spellbound. But she still wondered, "What if he was just a connoisseur of playing hearts? After all, he loved playing cards. Or what if he was the light in her darkness, could he really illuminate the depths of her soul?"

At this juncture she had the infinite patience for the moment of truth. Well, let's just say there wasn't denying she was completely awed. The recital was followed by a candlelit dinner, a bottle of sparkling vintage wine and white chocolate, exactly as Tusoli loved it. Jonathan hoped that the luxurious evening would revive the faculties that he knew must have been failing between them. All these dissipated some of her preceding belligerence but not enough to quell her cynicism towards his eccentricity.

Jonathan smiled, relieved to finally have the opportunity to explain himself. "I'm glad you understand, love," he said as he took a sip of his wine.

"I just wanted to do something special for you. And I hope you know that I would never intentionally leave you hanging like that."

Tusoli nodded and took a sip of her own wine, feeling the tension between them slowly dissipating, "I know," she said, looking into his eyes. "And I appreciate it. This is really amazing, Jonathan. Thank you."

They clinked their glasses together and settled into their dinner, enjoying each other's company and the romantic atmosphere of the cafe. They merrily ate and chatted, and Tusoli realized that she had misjudged Jonathan's intentions, and that his quirky behavior was simply a result of his desire to make her happy.

While indulging in the ambience of the candlelit dinner, Tusoli's ears perked up at the sound of music from a band playing in the bar area.

Suddenly, she recognized the song and exclaimed, "Wait a second, is that ...*Clotilda's on Fire by Shemekia Copeland?* Oh my God!"

Jonathan was surprised and responded, "I thought you wouldn't recognize it, wow."

Tusoli replied, "How could I not? I've listened to that song on repeat on YouTube since my mom told me about *The Clotilda.*"

Tusoli's head swiveled towards the source of the sound, and she saw the band playing on a small stage in the corner of the coffee bar.

Excitedly, Tusoli stood up and made her way to the bar area where she sang along with the two-piece band. The music was soulful and bluesy, and the lead singer's voice was deep and powerful.

It was a rendition of "*Clotilda's on Fire*" by *Shemekia Copeland,* a song that Tusoli truly loved because of the emotion it gave her. She was so caught up in the music that she almost forgot that Jonathan was sitting across the bar. Standing in front of the band, Tusoli swayed gently to the rhythm of the music. She felt completely absorbed in the moment, as if the rest of the world had disappeared and there was nothing but the music and the feeling it evoked. Tusoli started to sing along with the band and her voice blended in seamlessly with the music, and the audience was enraptured by her performance. Jonathan watched from afar, admiring her confidence and beauty as she sang along. Her lips moved with ease, mouthing the lyrics of the song as she became lost in the moment.

"Across the seas
Stormy waters
Showed no mercy
She was Satan's daughter"
Clotilda's on fire
Off the Alabama coast
Clotilda's on fire
We're still livin' with her ghost
She was a dirty secret

Forgotten, but not forgiven
But the shame was so great
She could not stay hidden
She's on fire"

Tusoli's voice filled the bar, carrying the weight of the lyrics and the emotion behind them. She poured her heart out with every note and Jonathan couldn't help but feel captivated by her performance. The band played along, matching her energy and passion. The other patrons at the bar were also entertained, with some even clapping and singing along.

"Her flame no longer lights up at night
Now dreams survive and hope burns bright
People still come from miles around
To praise the folks of Africa town
Who rose from the ashes of sad history
To stand unchained proud and free"
"Born to steal
With bodies to sell
She had her own special
Place in hell
Clotilda's on fire
Off the Alabama coast
Clotilda's on fire
We're still livin' with her ghost
She took souls
On a horrible trip
Her morning song
Was the crack of a whip
Ones who survived
Died a long time ago
Most of them buried
Out at old plateau"

She became one with the melody. Her eyes closed in blissful abandon, she surrendered herself completely to the spellbinding of the song. For a moment, the world around her dissolved into nothingness, and there was only the music and the feeling it inspired. And as the music swelled to a crescendo, the band let her sing the last of it.

"Clotilda's on fire
Off the Alabama coast
Clotilda's on fire
We're still livin' with her ghost
Clotilda's on fire
Off the Alabama coast
Clotilda's on fire
We're still livin'
We're still livin'
With her ghost"

This was a song that spoke to her soul, evoking memories and emotions that stirred deep within her. Jonathan walked over to her, his eyes gleaming with admiration, "You are amazing, Tusoli," he whispered, his voice full of sincerity. "I had no idea you could sing like that."

"Thanks, Jonathan. I love that song, it always brings out so much emotion in me."

And in that perfect moment, Jonathan hugged her tightly as Tusoli wrapped her arms around him with so much passion for the first time. Their embrace was so ecstatic, and everything seemed to freeze for a moment. The world was all theirs to conquer. He had got under the armor of her love at last, and he could feel her heart throb and writhe at each string that the band drove home. The intense yearning in his heart threatened any minute to burst forth into poetry. If only her burning desire could be poured out upon him, he would experience shockwaves so vehement and deeper than those caused into the earth by the thunderbolts of heaven.

When the band finally reeled the last string, the small audience erupted into cheers and applause, with Jonathan clapping the loudest. Tusoli felt exhilarated, as if she had just released a pent-up emotion that had been building up for years. She turned around to see Rudolph standing behind her, looking stunned and a bit embarrassed. Tusoli felt a wave of embarrassment wash over her too, but Jonathan quickly stepped in, introducing himself to Rudolph and offering him a drink. Tusoli winced from the paresthesia in her legs and she finally took back to her seat and watched as the two men exchanged pleasantries, trying to gauge Rudolph's reaction to the whole scene.

Eventually, the three of them sat down at the table and ordered some drinks. As they settled at the cozy set up, the clinking of glasses and hum of conversation surrounded them. Rudolph, Tusoli's godfather, greeted them with a warm smile, acknowledging her cheerful demeanor.

"Tusoli, I see you're having a really good time," he remarked.

Tusoli returned his smile and turned to introduce Jonathan to Rudolph officially.

"Hey Rudolph, meet Jonathan, my boyfriend," she said beaming with excitement.

Jonathan shook Rudolph's hand again, giving him a hearty but firm greeting. "My pleasure, Mr. Rudolph. I'm Jonathan," he said politely.

Tusoli continued with the introductions and shared a little bit about Rudolph's relationship with her family.

"Jonathan, Rudolph is my godfather. He was my dad's best friend back in the army before he passed on. He's also my best friend Karina's dad," she explained.

As soon as Jonathan heard this, he appeared to fall back into deep thought. His face took on a troubled expression, and he appeared to be ruminating on something. Tusoli couldn't help but feel concerned about his reaction.

"What's the matter, Jonathan? Is everything okay?" Tusoli asked, worriedly.

Jonathan let out a small sigh before responding, "It's nothing, Tusoli. I was just surprised to learn about Rudolph's connection to your family."

Tusoli could tell there was more to his reaction than he was letting on, but she didn't press the issue. Instead, she changed the subject and tried to steer the conversation towards lighter topics. There was a clear disquiet expression in his countenance and he was unable to maintain equanimity during the trialogue. He seemed a little distressed and quieter than usual as if some sort of reality had dawned upon him, but at least he was exonerated from the accusation of cheating. Tusoli found herself feeling more at ease, enjoying the company of both Jonathan and her godfather Rudolph. The rest of the evening passed in a blur of laughter, good food and wine, and the occasional musical performance from the band.

When the night came to a close, Tusoli found herself feeling grateful for the unexpected turn of events. She had come to the café with doubts and reservations, but now she felt like she had found a kindred spirit in Jonathan, and maybe even in Rudolph too. As Rudolph left the Cafe, he was proud of Tusoli. He had always known this girl was magic, and lucky was the man that got to keep her, but owe unto him that would get to lose her, he would experience the turmoil and tumult of never going a day without thinking about her.

Tusoli stood at the front door of her house, watching Jonathan ride off into the night on his Harley. She could still feel the vibrations of the powerful engine in her bones, and she couldn't help but smile at the memory of the ride. As she entered her house, she felt a mix of excitement and nervousness. Things were moving quickly with Jonathan, and she was not sure where it was all headed. But for now, she was content to let things unfold and see where that wild ride would take her.

She eventually got ready for bed, unable to stop replaying the events of the evening in her mind. From the moment she first saw Jonathan in the café, playing her a well-thought-out recital, to their exhilarating motorcycle ride, to the tender goodnight kiss, it all felt like a dream. As she drifted off to sleep, she knew it was all real, and she couldn't wait to see what adventures awaited her and Jonathan in the days, weeks, and years to come.

CHAPTER 6
THE NEW APARTMENT

On a bright yet crisp Saturday afternoon in Africatown, Mobile County, Jonathan and Tusoli were fully occupied with the daunting task of unpacking and settling into his new abode. The two were diligently coordinating the placement of various household items in the living room. Jonathan's new domicile, a snug two-bedroom apartment, was situated in the heart of the bustling city of Mobile.

While going through his possessions, Tusoli observed that Jonathan appeared to be grappling with the task of finding a suitable spot for his beloved vinyl record collection. With a frown on his face, Jonathan sighed heavily as he sorted through his stack of records. Tusoli, who had been organizing his books on the shelf, couldn't help but notice his frustration.

"What's wrong, Jonathan?" she asked.

"It's these records," he replied, holding up a few vinyl records.

"I don't know where to put them. I want to be able to see them, but I don't want them taking up too much space."

Tusoli walked over to him and took a closer look. She noticed that the records were mostly classic rock and jazz albums, and she smiled.

"You know, my dad had a similar collection," she said. "He used to keep them in a crate, so he could flip through them easily."

Jonathan's eyes lit up, "That's a great idea!" he exclaimed. "Do you think we could find a nice wooden crate to store them in?"

Tusoli nodded, "Sure, we could check out some thrift stores or antique shops. Maybe we'll find something that fits the vibe of your apartment."

Jonathan grinned, "Thanks, Tusoli. You always know how to make things work."

With enthusiasm, they continued unpacking and organizing, with Tusoli suggesting creative ways to make the apartment feel more like a home. They spent the next few hours organizing the apartment. Tusoli put up some pictures on the wall and arranged some decorative items on the shelves, while Jonathan hung some curtains and set up his record player in its new spot. By the end of the day, they had transformed the space into a cozy and inviting haven, filled with personal touches that reflected Jonathan's personality and style. Tusoli looked over at Jonathan and smiled,

"How does it feel to have your own place?" she asked.

"Amazing," Jonathan replied, taking her hand in his. "I can't imagine being anywhere else."

They sat on the sofa in comfortable silence for a few moments, enjoying the warmth of the sun streaming through the window.

Finally, Jonathan spoke up, "You know what would make this perfect? Some music."

Tusoli grinned, "I thought you'd never say it."

She got up and went over to the record player, carefully selecting an album and placing it on the turntable. The jazz music filled the room while Tusoli and Jonathan leaned back on the couch and let the sounds wash over them, feeling content and happy in the new house.

"Don't leave, we can spend the night here. Plus it's getting dark, I'm not sure it would be safe for you to go home right now." Jonathan urged Tusoli, who kept checking the time.

Tusoli replied, "My mum would be furious, I never spend nights away from home Jonathan."

"Well, there's always a first time, my love," Jonathan countered.

Tusoli hesitated, "I don't know, I gotta call my mom."

Helena's voice came from Tusoli's phone, "Hey Tusoli, still at Jonathan's new apartment? Have you guys finished unpacking?"

"Hey, mom, not yet?" Tusoli replied.

"Why don't you stay the night? You must be so tired," Helena suggested.

"Wait, what? Are you okay with that?" Tusoli asked in surprise.

"Come on Tusoli, you're a big girl now, you can make your own decisions. Plus, he's your boyfriend, right? After what he did for you last weekend, just help him out. I know you Tusoli, and I can never worry when it comes to the decisions you make," Helena reassured her daughter.

"Thank you for trusting me, mum. Have a good night. I'll see you tomorrow evening," Tusoli said gratefully.

"Told you, Helena wouldn't have a problem even if you move in with me," Jonathan remarked.

"My mum trusts you, and I always trust her intuition. She also trusts me, so I'll stay the night. She'll definitely have a problem if I move in with you Jonathan," Tusoli explained.

"Well, why don't we start with a small celebration? I've got some sweet wine," Jonathan suggested.

"Are you a connoisseur of wines or something? Because you always have wine," Tusoli joked.

"Well, because I know you love wine," Jonathan replied with a smile.

"No objection, sir. Bring the wine, but before that, I've got to take a quick shower." Tusoli begged.

"The shower is all yours, ma'am. I'll get you a towel. Feel at home," Jonathan replied with a grin.

Tusoli took the soft, fluffy towel that Jonathan offered, and gracefully made her way into the bathroom, which boasted an all-white tiled interior. As the hazy glass door slid shut behind her, a symphony of sound began to emanate from within—the dulcet patter of water droplets, each one playing its part in a soothing melody as it cascaded over Tusoli's honey-colored skin, slipping through her fingers and disappearing into the floor drain below.

Jonathan sank into the cushions of the sofa, listening intently to the tranquil notes of the shower, patiently waiting for her to emerge, like a butterfly from a cocoon, renewed and refreshed. The sound of the shower grew louder, and Jonathan's mind began to wander to Tusoli's bath time ritual. He couldn't help but picture the water cascading over every inch of her bare skin, droplets creating a glittering trail as they rolled down her curves. The thought alone made him ache with desire.

He couldn't help but feel a twinge of envy towards the water that had the privilege of touching her so intimately, caressing her honey-colored skin with each gentle drop. Oh, how he longed to be that close to her, to feel her warmth against his own skin.

In his imagination, he envisioned the luxurious lavender shower gel, its subtle fragrance enveloping her, nourishing her skin and leaving it soft and supple to the touch. He yearned to be the one to pamper her, to explore every inch of her body with his own hands, to witness the way her bare curves would dance beneath his fingertips.

And oh, the walls of that bathroom, how fortunate they were to bear witness to her beauty, to see her in all her glory from every possible angle. He couldn't help but envy them, as they contained the secrets of her form, while he had only ever caught fleeting glimpses of her thighs through the slit in her dress. Yet despite his longing, he knew he could never truly possess her, for she was as elusive as a fleeting dream, leaving him with nothing but the memory of her tantalizing presence. But today, perhaps things would be different. Perhaps the gods will be on his side. Perhaps, just perhaps, he will finally feel the soft caress of her skin against his own. Who knows? This mere thought made his heart ache with desire, longing for a moment of intimacy that had eluded him for far too long.

Jonathan was amused by his imagination of Tusoli in her bare skin, the allure hidden beneath her clothing, which only hinted at her African curves through those blue rugged jeans and corn dresses she adored. And at that moment, he silently crawled and stood in front of the blurry bathroom glass door, the only barrier between him and her, providing him with the pleasure and irresistible excitement of having a glimpse, albeit blurred, of all her curves.

Tusoli's silhouette behind the blurry glass door was like an abstract painting. Jonathan couldn't help but feel a flutter in his chest as he imagined her bare skin, wet and glistening under the cascading water. Each drop that splashed against her honey colored skin was a tease to his senses, igniting a spark of desire that made him yearn for her touch. He couldn't help but listen to the sound of the water, imagining it was him running his hands down her curves, tracing every contour and exploring every inch of her exquisite body. Time slowed to a crawl as he waited for her, his heart beating faster with each passing moment.

After a year of unrelenting pursuit, Jonathan had finally succeeded in bringing Tusoli into his grip. Yet, this sense of accomplishment felt vague and hollow, as he gazed upon her curves with a mix of desire and uncertainty. He yearned to feel her skin against his, to hold her in his arms as they slept. But for now, he could only revel in the tantalizing glimpses offered by the blurry bathroom door.

With each passing moment, his anticipation mounted, fueled by the knowledge that she was just on the other side of that frosted glass, and that he would soon have her all to himself. Jonathans' thoughts were interrupted by the sound of the shower turning off. He quickly rushed back to the couch and composed himself to greet Tusoli as she emerged from the bathroom, her skin glowing and her hair damp and tousled.

"Feeling better?" he asked, trying to keep his voice steady.

Tusoli smiled and nodded, wrapping the loose towel tightly around her body.

"Much better, thanks."

She borrowed a pair of Jonathan's pants and a t-shirt, to which he happily obliged. He sat on the couch, impatiently waiting for her return, again. She had disappeared into the bedroom to change, and when she reappeared, dressed in his clothes, Jonathan couldn't help but be amused by the sight of her. This was the closest he had ever come to touching her bare skin, even if it was just through the fabric of his own clothes. Tusoli quickly prepared a delectable plate of noodles sautéed with onions and butter for dinner. With a smile, she served Jonathan a portion, and he took a bite.

"Thank you so much. It's a simple dish, but you made it to perfection. It's been a while since I've tasted something this delicious. I'm really grateful," Jonathan remarked.

"You are welcome, that's just a tip of the iceberg" she replied with a beautiful smile.

"Well, that's why I can't wait to spend my life with you, I want the whole iceberg" He added while she blushed it away.

The two lovebirds sat on the couch, savoring their meal and sipping on the fine wine, the background music slowly fading into oblivion, leaving behind a conspicuous realm of silence. In that moment, you could hear the systole and diastole of their throbbing hearts, pounding in unison with an undeniable intensity. Jonathan's hand moved with a feather-like touch, wrapping around Tusoli's neck as his fingers trailed along her hair with tender care. She leaned back into him, feeling overwhelmed with emotion. This was the first time she had ever been this close to a man, and the sensation was both exhilarating and nerve-wracking.

As Jonathan's lips met her neck, a shiver coursed down her spine, sending her senses reeling. The unfamiliar sensation of his touch elicited a response from her body that she could barely contain. She was caught between wanting more and wanting him to stop. Her arms involuntarily clang to him as her heart thudded uncontrollably against his chest. Jonathan was keenly aware of the electric chemistry between them, and in a moment of impulsiveness, she wrapped her arms around his waist, their lips meeting in a soul-stirring kiss. It lasted for what seemed like eternity, more than ten seconds, and nearly gave away the depth of their feelings for each other.

In the midst of their intense emotional connection, Jonathan briefly paused to undo his belt. His sudden movement jolted Tusoli out of her emotional trance. It was at that moment that her eyes flew open in shock, and she quickly regained her senses, realizing what was happening. She quickly jumped up from the couch and backed away, her heart racing with a mixture of fear and confusion.

The moment that felt so right just seconds ago now felt shockingly wrong, and she couldn't understand how she had let things go so far. Her mind was in turmoil, and she struggled to come to terms with her conflicting feelings of desire and hesitation. Jonathan sat there, confused and unsure of what had just happened, and watched as Tusoli retreated to the other end of the sofa. Her voice quivered with emotion as she spoke, "Jonathan, I cannot go through with this."

Jonathan's expression contorted into a sneer as he retorted, "What? Why not? Have I done something wrong?"

Tusoli shook her head gently, "No, Jonathan. It's not about that. I simply don't believe I am ready for this."

Jonathan's desperation rose as he interrupted her,

"But Tusoli, my love for you is unchanging. Please, just let me make love to you."

Tusoli held her ground resolutely, "No, Jonathan. I cannot. Am not ready for this. Not today."

Jonathan, moving closer to her, realized that persuading her would not be easy. Yet he couldn't resist leaning in gently and kissing her once more; but her body stiffened as his lips touched hers again. She gently pushed him away and stood up, putting some distance between them. "Stop, Jonathan," she said calmly, her voice barely above a whisper. "I need some space to think."

Jonathan's face contorted with frustration, but he didn't argue this time. He could see the turmoil in Tusoli's eyes, and he knew he had to give her the time and space she needed. And once again, here she was, as elusive as she had always been. Untouched and pure, yet he couldn't break through her defenses. But he was hopeful; he knew he still had the whole night to persuade her.

CHAPTER 7
THE UNEXPECTED BABY

It was a typical day at the pharmacy, and Jonathan was engrossed in his work when his phone rang, interrupting his concentration.

"Jonathan, I have some news for you. I think I'm pregnant," said the caller on the other end of the line, her voice laced with apprehension.

Jonathan's heart skipped a beat as he processed the news. "What? You're pregnant?" he exclaimed incredulously, a mix of shock and confusion written on his face.

"How could this happen? I thought you were utilizing some form of contraception."

The caller let out a deep sigh before responding. "I was, but it must have failed. I don't know what to do, Jonathan. I need your help."

His features contorted into an expression of shock and disbelief, his mind racing with a million questions. His rapid heartbeat seemed to echo through the pharmacy as he struggled to maintain his composure. With a sense of urgency, he replied, "You can't tell anyone, not even your friends. We need to talk about this in person."

Jonathan's mind was already in overdrive, trying to come up with a solution to this unexpected news. He couldn't believe this was happening; not now, not when his life was finally back on track.

His phone rang again, but he refused to pick it up, consumed with anger and frustration. Jonathan paced back and forth, trying to collect his thoughts. The situation was dire, and he needed a plan. He had to figure out how to handle this bombshell without it blowing up in his face.

Chris, his colleague, who overheard him, walked in and immediately sensed something was off. "Seems like you got a girl pregnant, huh?" he said, grinning slyly.

"This is so messed up, man," Jonathan replied, his face contorted with emotion.

Chris arched an eyebrow. "You love her, don't you? I don't think it's a bad thing. The girl is strikingly beautiful; I saw her when she came looking for you some time back."

"Shut up, Chris. You don't understand," Jonathan snapped.

Chris leaned in his tone, serious," So, you don't want her to keep the baby?"

Jonathan exclaimed, "She can't keep this baby, Chris. And how do I even know it is mine? I'm just starting out this job, it's not even been a year. I can't be a parent now, Chris."

Chris asked, "What if she wants to keep it?"

Jonathan replied, "I have to convince her not to keep it. This can't be happening."

As Chris explained the legal ramifications of the situation, Jonathan's anxiety reached an all-time high. "I can't deal with this. I can't be in that baby mama court drama," he cried.

"How about I cover for you and you go get some air? Go home, Jonathan. You are a mess right now," Chris offered.

Jonathan replied, "I really need that, Chris. Could you cover for me tomorrow too? I need to sort this mess out once and for all."

Chris nodded, "Okay, just don't do anything crazy."

Jonathan's heart was racing as he dashed out of the pharmacy, the weight of the possibility of being a father crushing down on him. This wasn't supposed to be his life plan. He trudged through the rest of the day in a fog of confusion and disquiet, trying to make sense of it all.

Finally, after hours of internal struggle at his apartment, he picked up the phone and dialed Tusoli's number, his heart racing,

"Hey, when can we meet?" he asked, trying to keep the desperation out of his voice.

Tusoli's response was hesitant, "Hey, when?" she repeated.

"Tomorrow? I mean we could have dinner or something," Jonathan suggested, hoping she wouldn't push back.

But Tusoli did, "Not sure about tomorrow, could you not wait until the weekend? My leave starts this coming week and we had agreed already."

Jonathan's urgency grew, "Well, this is urgent, could you ask for a day or two off?"

Tusoli's voice was filled with skepticism, "Am in Auburn Jonathan, not Africatown, remember? What's so urgent it can't wait?"

Thinking on his feet, Jonathan made a quick decision, "Well, how about I come down to Auburn?"

Tusoli paused for a moment before conceding, "Tomorrow? Fine, that would work. Is everything okay?"

Jonathan's heart sank, "See you tomorrow. Nothing to worry about," he lied.

Tusoli seemed unconvinced but agreed, "Okay, I'll be waiting."

Jonathan had no clue what he was doing, but he had to fix this festering mess he landed himself into. He always thought he had everything under control but he was now faced with one of the most intractable tests on his disposition.

AT 10 A.M., JONATHAN set off on a three-hour drive to Auburn, Alabama, the morning sun casting long shadows on the empty highway. The road stretched out before him, a ribbon of asphalt winding through dense forests and rolling hills, as he hoped against hope that everything would work out between him and Tusoli.

As he drove, the landscape gradually shifted from the vibrant greens of the countryside to the quaint charm of Auburn, where historic buildings and towering oaks lined the streets. Upon arrival, he pulled into a small, welcoming hotel, its brick facade and blooming flower boxes exuding Southern hospitality.

Jonathan checked in, the receptionist's warm smile doing little to ease his anxious mind. The room was simple yet cozy, with sunlight filtering through lace curtains and casting delicate patterns on the walls. He placed his bag on the neatly made bed and took a deep breath, steeling himself for what was to come. With a mixture of anticipation and nervousness, Jonathan dialed Tusoli's number, the phone's ringing echoing the beat of his anxious heart.

"I just checked into a hotel here in Auburn. Can we meet after work? Meanwhile, I'll explore the city," Jonathan texted, his fingers tapping nervously on the screen.

Tusoli responded quickly, "Sure, see you later. Auburn has some stunning views and beautiful girls."

Jonathan smiled at her playful tone but knew that beneath it, Tusoli was likely surprised. He could imagine her expressive eyes widening in disbelief as she read his message. After all, he had driven all the way to Auburn just to see her. She hadn't expected him to make such a long trip to her workplace, where she served as an ENT specialist at a private medical facility. For the past three months, she had been working there after her application was accepted. Despite the decent pay, Tusoli preferred to stay with her grandfather, who was more than happy to host her.

Their long-distance relationship had its fair share of ups and downs since she moved to Auburn, but the prospect of seeing Jonathan filled her with excitement. As she left work, her phone rang. It was her mom.

"Hi darling, how are you and how's work? We haven't talked in days," Helena's voice was warm and familiar.

"Hey mom, I was just about to call you. It's been crazy, but I am coping well. So, no worries... guess who just showed up in Auburn," Tusoli replied, her voice tinged with excitement.

Helena laughed softly, "Who else would that be? Jonathan?"

"Yeah, I'm just heading out to meet him," Tusoli chuckled, feeling a flutter of joy.

"Well, how about we talk tomorrow and you can tell me all about it," Helena suggested.

"Okay, mom. Bye. I love you," Tusoli said, her heart light.

After hanging up, she quickly called Jonathan to find his location. "Hey, where are you?" she asked, stepping out into the golden afternoon light.

"There's this beautiful place called Skybar, find me there," Jonathan replied, his voice filled with anticipation.

Tusoli arrived shortly at the Skybar Cafe. She spotted Jonathan sitting at the bar, his eyes searching the room for her. When their eyes met, he stood up, a huge smile spreading across his face. Tusoli rushed to him, and they embraced tightly, their bodies fitting together perfectly. The passion between them was undeniable, and they shared a lingering kiss, savoring the closeness they had missed.

"Welcome to Auburn," Tusoli exclaimed with a wide, anxious smile.

Jonathan couldn't help but notice how her face lit up when she saw him. "Thank you, my love," he replied, his voice warm. "I'm already in love with Auburn," he added, his eyes twinkling.

"Well, no one who loves this city ever forgets her, so you're cuffeHere's a refined version of the passage:

"For life, you say? That sounds like something I'd do to you," Jonathan replied, his laughter filling the air with warmth.

Tusoli's playful smile faded, replaced by a serious expression. "What brings you to Auburn? You weren't so nice the last time we talked on the phone after I broke the news to you. In fact, you hung up on me. Did you really just come to see me, or to break up with me?"

Jonathan met her gaze, his expression earnest. "I'm sorry for how things turned out between us. It's been hard to cope without you in Africatown," he admitted. "I had hoped we could move in together, but then you left. That's why I moved out from my parents' place. I wanted to be with you, remember?"

"We made a commitment to support each other, Jonathan," Tusoli said gently, her voice softening. "I couldn't pass up this job opportunity. Plus, my mom was ecstatic to see me finally making progress in my life."

She took a deep breath, looking at his face. "How about we find you a job here in Auburn? There are many opportunities for a competent pharmacist like you, and I'm happy to assist you with the application process."

Jonathan looked touched by her offer. "You really think I could find something here?

Tusoli nodded, a reassuring smile spreading across her face. "I know you can. Auburn could be a fresh start for both of us."

As they sat at the bar, the noise of the café faded into the background, leaving only their heartfelt conversation and the promise of a shared future ahead.

Jonathan's eyes lit up with excitement, "I have always dreamed of starting our life together since we graduated from college, and I can't wait any longer. I'm done waiting, Tusoli."

His words resonated with determination and passion, stirring something deep within Tusoli. Despite her skepticism, she couldn't deny the sincerity in his voice. Her heart fluttered nervously as she searched his eyes for reassurance.

"What changed, Jonathan? You were breaking up with me on the phone just the other day," she said softly, her guard still up from their recent conversation. She needed to be sure he wasn't going to hurt her again.

Jonathan took her hands gently in his, his gaze unwavering. "I know I messed up, Tusoli. I let my fears get the best of me. But being apart from you made me realize how much I need you in my life," he confessed earnestly. "I've had time to think, and I want to make things right between us. I want us to build our future together, here in Auburn."

Tusoli studied his face, seeing the sincerity and vulnerability he rarely showed. A wave of conflicting emotions washed over her—fear, hope, and a flicker of renewed trust. She squeezed his hands gently, her voice barely above a whisper. "Jonathan, I want to believe you. I want to believe that we can make this work."

Jonathan nodded fervently, his grip tightening slightly on her hands. "We can, Tusoli. I'm committed to making it work, no matter what it takes," he promised, his voice filled with conviction.

"Hey, look, my love," Jonathan continued, gently holding Tusoli's hand in his. "I know I was a little selfish and maybe hard on you. I just didn't think you wanted me as bad as I wanted you."

Tusoli felt a small smile start to form on her lips. "Of course I want you, Jonathan," she said softly, squeezing his hand. "But I need to know that we're both in this together. No more misunderstandings or doubts."

Jonathan nodded earnestly. "I understand, Tusoli. And I promise to do better. I don't want to lose you."

"I know you got a little distant after that night we moved into your new apartment," Tusoli continued, her voice gentle. "Honestly, I've never been that passionate with another human being my whole life."

"We just couldn't have sex, Jonathan," Tusoli added, looking down at her hands. "I really wanted more of that, and I've thought about that night every day since... but I needed to be ready. I hope you understand."

"I understand," Jonathan said softly, his thumb tracing comforting circles on the back of her hand. "But I want you to know that I'm willing to take things slow if that's what you need. I just know that I want to be with you."

Tusoli looked at Jonathan expectantly. "Well, I'm right here. You hold the key to us, Jonathan," she said quietly. "So why did you actually come, just to say sorry?"

Jonathan took a deep breath, meeting her gaze with unwavering sincerity. "No, not just to say sorry," he said earnestly. "I came to tell you that I want to be with you, Tusoli. I want to work things out between us and be the partner that you deserve."

The wedding bells
Tusoli Thandi Tolewa.
This is the day the bells ring
I have come to give you this diamond ring
On my bended knee
I ask with much anticipation
That you will not say no to this life I envision.
I didn't sleep last night
You were right in my sight
I played it all over again, I was a total mess
And in my script I knew you would say Yes.
I didn't know how to scheme it out
I was afraid you would scream or shout
I was dying with anxiety and unknown fear
If you say No, how will I move on from here.
Am weary of waiting until the day I'll be ready
Am in incessant torment please be my remedy
From this day I want you for more than eternity

Without you everything is just but vanity.
You are my soulmate, am your knight
For all the wrongs I will make it right
And when your hands grow feeble
My virtue is I will be at your elbow.
My therapist for a world filled with conflict
Like thunder I'll pour on those that afflict
What if am ready but you are Not
What if this is the only chance that we've got.

Like a Knight in front of their lord, as a display of respect, love, and loyalty, Jonathan went down on one knee, holding a ring box in his left hand and opened it with his right hand, revealing a gorgeous Diamond engagement ring for Tusoli and called her by her three names, "Tusoli Thandi Tolewa, will you marry me."

Tusoli's eyes widened in shock, her heart racing with unexpected joy. The crowd in the café erupted into cheers, urging her to say yes. In a whirlwind of emotions, she flashed back to all the beautiful moments they had shared. Without hesitation, a smile of pure bliss spread across her face.

"Yeees, Jonathan, I have been waiting for this day all my life!" Tusoli exclaimed, overwhelmed with happiness.

In no time, the café erupted into celebration, marked with showers of confetti, a popped bottle of champagne, lively music, and delicious food. Tusoli was ecstatic, and she would do anything for Jonathan on this night. She knew without a doubt that he was the man she would spend the rest of her life with.

Tusoli couldn't take her eyes off the stunning diamond ring on her finger. It looked perfect, and she regarded it with wonder and pleasure as she danced around Jonathan, feeling his arms wrap around her, his hands lapping her curves as they moved in harmony.

This was Auburn, it was full of life, good wine and good music, and Tusoli had never experienced it this way. It was a wild and crazy night at the club, the bass was thumping, the drinks were flowing, and the energy was electric. Tusoli was ready to let loose and have a good time for once in her life. She was eager to let go and enjoy herself like never before. That night, they wandered through the lively streets of Auburn and animated avenues discovering its effervescent nightlife.

They visited an array of eclectic art cafes, their hands intertwined, and their steps matching the beat of the starry night. Tusoli, captivated by the moment, couldn't resist planting random kisses on Jonathan's lips. They engaged in meaningful conversations and swayed to the rhythm of the music wherever they went, reveling in the joys of the night. Tusoli even belted out her favorite tunes, her voice often lost amid the blaring music of the various nightclubs they patronized. It was a night that would be etched in her memory forever, as if it were their last on earth.

For Jonathan, Tusoli's alluring nature had never shone brighter. With each passing moment, he found himself captivated by her enigmatic essence, as if peeling away layers of her persona like an onion, revealing new facets of her personality one by one. Yet, there was a sense of mystique to her that continued to elude him, leaving him eager to uncover the depths of her complexities. Only time would tell if he would be fortunate enough to experience her in all her entirety.

Twilight approached, and the sky began to take on a dusky hue, Tusoli and Jonathan, drained from the night's excitement, stumbled back to the hotel. Jonathan's head was spinning from the tequila and wine he had imbibed, his steps unsteady. When they reached their room, they collapsed onto the bed, their bodies sinking into the soft mattress. Exhausted but content, they lay intertwined, lost in the aftermath of their whirlwind of emotions and experiences.

Tusoli's phone buzzed and woke her up. She groggily looked at the screen and saw that it was already 10 a.m. Panic surged through her as she realized she was an hour late for work. Her head throbbed from the wine she drank the night before, and she struggled to recall the events of the night. Nudging Jonathan, she noticed his phone lighting up with missed calls from his boss and Chris. Jonathan, too, was supposed to have reported back to work, but instead, he found himself in a hotel room in a city three hours away. As the reality sank in, they exchanged nervous glances, realizing they were in for a rough morning.

With time running short, the pair sprang into action. Jonathan cast aside the rumpled sheets and frantically asked, "I need to take a shower, and where are my car keys?"

"We have no time for showers, Jonathan," Tusoli retorted, her voice laced with urgency. "I'm already an hour late for work, and I could lose my job. Here are your keys. Let's go."

Tusoli rushed out in a flurry, her heart pounding with anxiety over the possibility of losing her job. Jonathan followed closely behind, his mind racing with thoughts of how he could help her fix the situation. As they reached the car, Jonathan realized he had almost left his luggage behind at the hotel reception. Thankfully, the attentive staff had noticed and brought it to the car just in time. Meanwhile, Tusoli dashed to a nearby clothing store, determined to find something suitable to wear for work. With no time to spare, she hastily selected a new dress, the urgency of the moment adding an unexpected thrill to their chaotic morning.

"Can you drop me off?" Tusoli asked Jonathan.

"Of course," Jonathan replied with a warm smile. "I love the dress. Blue looks good on you."

"Thank you. How did we fall asleep last night? You were so drunk," Tusoli asked, concern lacing her voice.

"I don't know. I guess I had too much tequila," Jonathan admitted with a sheepish grin. "I got a great deal of missed calls from Chris and my supervisor. I really need to hit the road."

Tusoli nodded understandingly. "It's okay, Jonathan. Just take care of yourself, alright?"

Jonathan glanced at her, his eyes reflecting gratitude. "Thanks, Tusoli. I'm lucky to have you."

With nimble haste, they arrived at Tusoli's place of work. Jonathan parted from her with a tender kiss before embarking on the long journey back to Mobile County. He chastised himself for drifting off to sleep and forfeiting his opportunity with the beautiful Tusoli the night before. This was the night Tusoli would have given all herself to him.

Weary and exhausted, he finally arrived at his workplace after a prolonged two-hour and twenty-minute drive. As he stepped out of his car, Jonathan couldn't shake off the feeling of regret. He couldn't stop thinking about the missed opportunity with Tusoli. They had shared a passionate night together in Auburn, and Tusoli had been ready to take their relationship to the next level. But Jonathan had been too drunk and had fallen asleep, missing out on the chance to be with her in the most intimate way possible.

The memory haunted him as he walked through the familiar doors of his workplace. He couldn't shake off the regret of not being able to fully express his love for Tusoli when she had been willing and eager. But as he began his day, Jonathan made a silent vow to himself: he wouldn't let another opportunity with Tusoli slip through his fingers, ever again.

Jonathan's arrival at work was however greeted with a summons to his supervisor's office, where disgruntlement for his absence loomed heavy in the air. Meanwhile, Tusoli was forced to make amends with the disgruntled patients waiting for her, and she devoted the remainder of the day to tending to their needs. She frequently gazed at the mesmerizing ring on her finger, eager to share the news with her mother.

CHAPTER 8
THE WEDDING PLANNER

"**D**o you, Jonathan Ansel Omondy, take this woman to be your lawfully wedded wife, to live together after God's ordinance in holy matrimony? Will you love her, comfort her, honor her, and keep her in sickness and in health; and forsaking all others, keep thee, only unto her, so long as ye both shall live?" The minister's voice rang out with solemnity, as Tusoli pictured her dream wedding ceremony.

"Did I say the words well, Karina?" Tusoli asked, a smile tugging at the corners of her lips.

"Perfectly well. I just came to confirm the engagement news," replied Karina, her eyes twinkling with excitement.

"Can you imagine? I'm getting married soon!" Tusoli gushed about the beautiful night. She recounted how Jonathan surprised her by driving all the way to Auburn, bringing a stunning diamond ring, and going down on one knee to ask her to marry him.

"That's wonderful! I'm so happy for you," exclaimed Karina, giving Tusoli a warm hug, "When's the big day?" she asked.

"We haven't decided yet," Tusoli replied with a smile. "We want to take our time and plan everything carefully." she added.

Karina nodded understandingly. "Well, whenever it is, count me in. I can't wait to see you as a bride."

Tusoli blushed, "Thank you, Karina. You're such a good friend."

As Tusoli narrated her engagement news, Karina looked at her with a mixture of joy and sadness. She had never seen her friend so happy, but at the same time, she couldn't help but feel a twinge of guilt and regret. They had been best friends since childhood and had grown up together, but lately, their friendship had changed. They had drifted apart and didn't talk as much anymore. Karina felt like she was just a *ghost* in front of Tusoli's eyes, merely a fleeting presence in her life, a distant memory of a time when they were inseparable.

Am a ghost

Am a ghost,

I Am lost

And you can't see through me,

I shout and scream but you can't hear me.

I am trapped in this dreaded tie,

I can't escape no matter how hard I try,

I need a hug but you pass me by,

I want to talk or I will die.

It's so empty inside here,

How did we forget how to laugh,

Yet you are right with me oh dear,

What happened to that beautiful girlish stuff?

When last did we go to movies or coffee,

We were girls, we were always goofy,

But now look at me am always gloomy,

Am a ghost and you can't see through me.

We've been through thick and thin,

You are the most honest I've seen,

But am sorry you don't know me,

Am a ghost. You can't see through me.

Tusoli's voice was filled with concern as she noticed Karina's distant expression, "Is everything alright, Karina? You seem a little preoccupied."

Karina sighed, "Am okay, It's just schoolwork, Tusoli. It's been taking up all of my time lately."

Tusoli nodded in understanding, "I know how that can be, but it feels like we haven't talked in a while. I miss our conversations. It seems like we've grown apart."

Karina hesitated before answering,

"I feel the same way, Tusoli. But it's just been hard to balance everything lately."

Tusoli placed a comforting hand on Karina's arm, "I understand. Just know that you can always talk to me about anything. We've been best friends forever, and that will never change."

(*The doorbell rang, and Tusoli rushed to answer it.*)

"I'll get that," she shouted.

"Hey, love! Look who's here! Karina, it's been ages since we've all hung out together," Helena exclaimed as she entered the house in high spirits.

Karina responded, "Hey, Helena. Actually, I was just about to leave."

"Don't be silly, Karina. You can't leave without catching up with us. Stay the night," Helena insisted.

Tusoli chimed in, "Yeah, stay over. It'll be a fun girls' night-in!"

Karina hesitated, "I wish I could, but I have an exam tomorrow and I need to study. Maybe another time?"

Tusoli nodded understandingly, "Oh, I understand. Good luck with your exam. Let's catch up soon."

Karina smiled, "Definitely. Goodnight, Tusoli, and goodnight, Helena."

"Goodnight," they both replied in unison.

Tusoli opened the door for Karina and gave her a gentle hug. Karina felt tense and worried, but Tusoli's comforting embrace brought a sense of calm.

"Don't worry, you'll be okay. Goodnight," Tusoli said reassuringly before closing the door and heading to the kitchen to help her mother make dinner. Helena noticed that Karina seemed different.

"Is Karina okay? She seems a little off," Helena asked, concern evident in her voice.

Tusoli nodded, "I'm not sure, Mum. She's been preoccupied with school lately, and she seemed a bit stressed when she arrived."

Helena gently suggested, "Maybe she's having some problems with her boyfriend?"

Tusoli shook her head, "I don't think so. Actually, I don't even know if they're still together. We haven't talked about that stuff in a while."

Helena reassured Tusoli, "You know one thing about childhood friends? They never stop being friends no matter what."

Tusoli smiled appreciatively, "You're right, Mum. I believe Karina will find her way."

Helena asked Tusoli if Jonathan was still planning to come for dinner the next day for the wedding planner, and Tusoli confirmed that he was indeed coming.

"Great, I can't wait to meet him," Helena said with genuine enthusiasm.

Tusoli then bid her mother goodnight, and Helena responded with a loving "Goodnight, baby."

As darkness fell, a wreath of clouds swirled in the night sky of Africatown, with distant thunder grumbling ominously. The drizzle outside intensified, and the circling shroud of the Storm rolled nearer. Within moments, the gentle pitter-patter transformed into a deafening roar as rain cascaded from the heavens. What began as light showers soon escalated into a relentless downpour, as if nature itself sought to cleanse the world of its odious pomps and vanities. It was as if the sky had opened up, unleashing its wrath upon the earth below. The rain pounded against Tusoli's roof, sounding like a thousand tiny drums playing all at once. Gutters overflowed, sending water cascading down the sides of the house in a torrential deluge. It seemed that the very heavens were weeping, unleashing their pent-up fury upon the world below.

Such a stormy night had not been witnessed in Africatown for a very long time.

CHAPTER 9
WHEN IT RAINS. IT POURS

The following morning dawned dull and dreary, with a persistent drizzle that soaked everything in a damp, heavy haze. The clouds hung low in the sky, casting a gray blanket over the world below. The air was cool and misty, and the atmosphere was heavy with a sense of ominous gloom. It felt as if the very essence of the storm from the night before still lingered, weighing down on everything with its somber presence.

His phone rang, and Jonathan answered with a sense of annoyance in his voice, "What is it?" he snapped, "I paid for the pills and everything else that was needed. We agreed that it was a mistake and we should get over it. I'm sorry you had to go through this."

The voice on the other end trembled with fear and despair.

"Jonathan, I can't do this anymore," she cried. "You have to come out clean. This is draining me and driving me nuts. The termination failed. I ran another scan and it revealed I'm now ten weeks pregnant, and it looks suspicious."

The weight of the situation finally dawned on Jonathan, and he felt his stomach drop. He knew he could no longer ignore the reality of what they had done. But before he could respond, the line went dead.

That evening, as Tusoli and her mother cooked a delicious meal for the groom-to-be, the doorbell rang. Tusoli rushed to answer it, a big smile lighting up her face.

"Hi Jonathan, welcome! We're so glad you could make it," she said, feeling a flutter of nerves as she greeted him.

Helena walked over to join them, giving Jonathan a warm hug. "Welcome, son."

"Thank you for having me over for dinner, it smells amazing in here," Jonathan said, looking around the kitchen.

"We made all your favorites. Hope you're hungry," Helena replied with a smile.

They took their seats at the dining table and began to enjoy the scrumptious meal that Tusoli and her mother had prepared before commencement of the wedding plans.

Just before they could start, the doorbell rang, prompting Helena to inquire if someone was expected. Tusoli explained that she had invited Karina, her best friend, to join them as she was a skilled planner they could make use of.

Jonathan felt uneasy and expressed his concerns, "I thought it was just us. I don't think it's a good idea to involve a friend just yet."

Tusoli reassured him, "It's alright, Karina is like family to me. We're trying to rekindle our friendship, and she's amazing at planning, you'll see."

Helena concurred and rushed to the door, excited to welcome Karina into their home once more.

Karina gently walked in, and Helena invited her to the well-orchestrated dining set filled with an abundance of food. As Helena went ahead to serve a plate of food, Karina paused for a second, her gaze piercing as she locked eyes with Jonathan without a single blink. Her lips curled in disdain, trying as much as possible to hold back her simmering temper. She looked at him, disgusted by his shallow decoy, as he slowly chewed his last mouthful of chicken. If looks could kill, her scowl would have slain Jonathan on the spot.

Tusoli noticed the scowling look and called her out. "Karina, what's wrong? Take a seat," she politely asked.

Karina answered, "No, Tusoli, I can't sit at the same table with this lunatic."

Helena, totally shocked, turned to look at her, while Tusoli was a little confused, now looking at Jonathan.

"Wait, what did you just say? What lunatic? You and Jonathan have met each other?" Tusoli asked, looking furious.

Helena came closer, "What's going on here?"

Karina responded in a firm tone, "Tell them, Jonathan, say it or I'll do it!"

Tusoli and Helena stared at Jonathan, dumbfounded.

"What's she talking about, Jonathan? Can you please say something?" Tusoli asked, confused.

Jonathan was startled, he never anticipated this sudden turn of events. He felt a knot form in his stomach as he searched for the right words, but they eluded him. Tusoli's gaze was like fire, burning into him, demanding answers.

Meanwhile, Karina's expression was inscrutable, her eyes flashing with a mix of anger and determination. She seemed poised to reveal something significant, something that would change everything.

Tusoli's patience was wearing thin. "Karina, what is going on? What do you mean by 'lunatic'?" she demanded, her voice tinged with a hint of desperation.

Helena, sensing the tension, stepped forward, her eyes darting between the three of them. "Yes, Karina, please, tell us what's going on," she urged, her voice barely above a whisper, but filled with anticipation.

Tusoli's voice was laced with urgency as she addressed Karina, her eyes darting between her best friend and Jonathan. "Karina, you need to tell us what's going on. Jonathan, please, say something," she demanded, her composure barely holding as she fought to make sense of the situation.

Helena's confusion mirrored Tusoli's, her brows furrowed in concern. "What's happening here? Why is everyone so tense?" she asked, looking from Karina to Jonathan and back again.

Karina took a deep breath, her voice steady as she delivered the bombshell. "I'll tell you," she began, her eyes fixed on Tusoli. "I'm pregnant, Tusoli. For Jonathan... he tried to convince me to have an abortion. But it didn't work."

"Whaat??", Tusoli declared. Her heart skipped a beat as Karina's words hung in the air, shattering the tranquility of the room. Her mind raced, trying to process the revelation, while her emotions churned like a stormy sea.

With a suffocating gasp, she fell back into the chair on which she was very well ensconced, her body feeling heavy and constricted, the weight of the revelation hitting her like a ton of bricks. Her body felt heavy, as if every muscle had turned to lead. With shaking hands, she covered her mouth trying to stifle the wave of dismay that threatened to overwhelm her. Beads of sweat began to form on her forehead, perhaps from the unrelenting heat from the kitchen or from the suffocating tension in the room. She was becoming more and more exasperated by the second. She was caught in a whirlwind of disbelief and despair, her mind reeling as she struggled to process the shocking truth.

Helena's eyes widened in shock, her hand flying to her mouth in disbelief. "Oh my God," she gasped, her voice trembling with emotion. "Jonathan, is this true?"

"I didn't quite understand, Karina. Are you saying that you are pregnant with Jonathan's baby? We were just making arrangements for the wedding, weren't we Jonathan?" Helena's voice trembled with disbelief as she turned to Jonathan, her eyes searching his face for any sign of denial or explanation. Jonathan, however, remained silent, his gaze fixed on the floor as if avoiding the weight of the accusation.

Tusoli's world seemed to crumble around her as the weight of the truth sank in. She felt a surge of anger, betrayal, and heartbreak all at once. She turned to Jonathan, her eyes blazing with fury. "How could you?" she demanded, her voice laced with venom. "How could you do this to me?"

Jonathan's face paled, his throat dry as he struggled to find the words. "I... I..." he stammered, his voice barely a whisper. But guilt was written all over his face, confirming Karina's accusation.

Tusoli was speechless and sat aghast, in a split of a second, she connected all the dots, piecing together the moments that now seemed tainted with betrayal. She looked at Jonathan with a mixture of disbelief and disgust, her trust in him shattered.

"Karina, where were you on my graduation day?" Tusoli's voice quivered with sadness.

"Jonathan had invited me to his party, he never told me you were close or anything," Karina responded defensively.

"And what about on the day we went to check out The Clotilda, where were you Karina?" Tusoli pressed, her voice tinged with accusation.

"I was with him. He brought me flowers and a poem, which I declined the previous evening. I did so because I suspected you two were a thing, but he wouldn't accept it," Karina explained, her tone filled with regret.

Helena raised her voice in surprise, "Wow, are those not the same flowers and the poem he brought you the following morning!"

"Karina, you never thought of sharing all of this with me? I thought we were best friends, Karina," Tusoli posed tearfully.

"And Jonathan, you are disgusting. How could you do this to me?" Tusoli burst into tears.

"Helena, Tusoli, Karina, I am really sorry, allow me to clarify," Jonathan implored, his hands folded gently over his chest.

"Sorry? Do you really think you can just say sorry and that's it? You made my best friend pregnant while I was away in Auburn, all faithful and waiting for my Jonathan! You cheated on me, Jonathan. I'd take that. But a baby? Really?!" Tusoli cried out, her voice filled with anger and betrayal.

She felt weak and helpless, as if her heart was shattering into a million pieces. It all seemed like a far-fetched theory, but with the evidence staring her in the face, she couldn't deny it

"Then you come and fool me with an engagement ring, making me believe that we will build a life together. You can go straight to hell, Jonathan!" Tusoli exclaimed with anger and heartbreak.

Helena was angered, her hands on her waist. "You know what, Jonathan, I am frankly disappointed in you. This is repugnant and absurd to say the least. Get out of my house right now!"

With a fierce grip, Helena seized Jonathan by the ear and yanked him forcefully from the dining table, causing glasses to crash and shatter, the cacophony of breaking glass filling the air like a symphony of chaos. She dragged him across the room, his protests drowned out by the crashing noise, until she flung him out of the door with a resounding thud. Jonathan stumbled backward, his eyes wide with shock as he landed hard on the ground, the rain soaking him to the bone. Helena stood in the doorway, her silhouette framed by the dim light, radiating an aura of righteous fury.

"You disgust me, Jonathan!" she thundered, her voice cutting through the air like a whip. "Get out of my home and never come back!"

Jonathan scrambled to his feet, his heart pounding in his chest as he stared back at Helena, unable to find the words to defend himself. The weight of his betrayal hung heavy around him, suffocating him with its enormity. He turned and fled into the night like a beaten thief, the rain pelting down on him like a relentless punishment, each drop a reminder of his shame. The thunder roared above, echoing the tumult of his inner turmoil, while lightning illuminated the darkness like a spotlight on his disgrace, as if the heavens themselves were condemning him for his sins.

Tusoli asked tearfully, "Karina, for how long has this been going on?"

Karina took a deep breath and replied, "I met him in college a year before you guys graduated, and we almost had something. But later on, I found out from my dad that you had introduced him as your boyfriend at the Cafeteria. He denied it when I confronted him. When you went to work in Auburn, he used to take me out, and sometimes I'd spend nights at his apartment."

Tusoli's tears turned into a mix of anger and despair as Karina's words sank in. She couldn't believe that Jonathan had been lying to her for so long, and that her best friend had been involved in the whole mess, and this finally explained her recent behavior.

"I can't even imagine what you must have gone through, Karina. And to think that he was using me as a cover this whole time," Tusoli said, her voice shaking with emotion.

"I'm so sorry, Tusoli. I didn't know how to tell you, and I didn't want to ruin our friendship," Karina replied, her own tears falling.

Tusoli steadied herself, her resolve hardening. "We need to confront him and make him face the consequences of his actions. We can't let him get away with this."

"But what about the wedding plans?" Karina asked, concern etched on her face.

Tusoli's jaw clenched. "The wedding is off. I can't marry someone who has betrayed my trust like this. We'll deal with the aftermath later, but right now, Jonathan needs to own up to what he's done."

Tusoli's tears flowed freely, her heart heavy with pain and betrayal. She couldn't stop the flood of emotions overwhelming her. Jonathan's deceit cut deep, shattering the trust she had placed in him. Alongside the pain, she grappled with guilt, questioning how she could have missed the signs and allowed this betrayal to unfold right under her nose, not just to her but to her best friend as well.

"Mum, was I too much for him? Or was I just not enough?" Tusoli's voice cracked as tears streamed down her face. "Did I have so many faults that he could do this to me?" She clutched her mum tightly, her heart aching with raw pain and confusion.

Helena stood beside Tusoli, her heart breaking for her daughter. She longed to offer words of comfort, but the weight of the situation left her speechless. All she could do was hold Tusoli close, hoping her presence would provide some solace in the midst of the turmoil.

Karina on the other hand was trachled. She stormed out in tears, feeling utterly betrayed and used. She came guns blazing into Jonathan's little love story, and in no time, she burnt everything to the ground. There were no words to express the depth of her agony. Jonathan was only interested in her charms, eager to make love to her in a philandering sort of way, without really intending to have any meaningful relationship with her, like she was only a sophomore in his bivouac, a pawn in his game, a mere placeholder in his life.

Tusoli was sickened and attenuated. She stumbled to the bathroom, tears blurring her vision as she doubled over the sink. Fluids regurgitated through her nose from all the crying, and her voice became nasal and indistinct. Taking a deep breath, she pulled back her hair and looked at herself in the bathroom mirror, her reflection distorted by tears and anguish. She was oblivious to the water overflowing over the sink, lost in her own turmoil.

The person in the mirror
We all crave to be loved
We sit and wait to be wanted
We often forget the person in the mirror.
We wait so much for one who's not deserved
We feed their demons just to be haunted
We so often forget the person in the mirror.
We give and love with all our being
There are none so blind in love as us who won't see
We so often forget the person in the mirror.
We make a home, we do everything
In their arms we think is where we'd rather be
We so often forget the person in the mirror.
So, what's in the end for us that wait?
How long is eternity?
We so often forget the person in the mirror.
How long can we carry this much weight?

What if it's nothing but vanity?
We have to learn to love the person in the mirror.

JONATHAN WAS ENGULFED in a tempest of emotions. His mind fell into a chaotic frenzy as he grappled with the dire aftermath of his transgressions. The once-gleaming horizon of his future with Tusoli had been eclipsed by the dark shadows of remorse, regret, and a haunting sense of loss. He had truly loved her with all his heart, and the mere thought of losing her to his folly was agonizing.

He sat slumped in his apartment, the world outside seeming a blur to him, his thoughts in a tumultuous whirlpool. He stared out of the window, lost in a sea of reflections, wondering if things could have been different if he had chosen a path of righteousness instead of indulging in temptation with Karina.

The weight of his actions was crushing, and he felt trapped in a web of his own making. The silence around him was deafening, a stark reminder of the void he had created in his life and in the life of the woman he loved. The ruins of his wedding plans and shattered future lay before him, a painful reminder of what he had truly lost.

The realization that his involvement with Karina had cost him the love of his life was a bitter pill to swallow. He was overcome with sorrow, the unrelenting pain and anguish of his body and mind crushing his once dauntless spirit. Jonathan found himself in the darkest depths of despair, with no lifeline to pull him from the abyss. He was consumed by utter misery.

He, however, knew that time was his ally, and he hoped that distance would soothe the ire of Tusoli's wrath. As he awaited her cooling off, he was haunted by the implications of his missteps. Karina and her baby added a new dimension to his predicament, and he was at a loss on how to handle the situation. He felt like a ship tossed in a tempestuous sea, at the mercy of the whims of fate. The storm clouds of uncertainty loomed over his future, and he felt powerless in the face of the destructive forces of his own making. Yet, in the midst of this chaos, he clung to a sliver of hope that somehow, someway, he could find redemption and rebuild what he had lost.

After a night of regret and agony, Jonathan arrived at his workplace the following morning. A sense of dread slowly crept up his spine. His premonition proved correct as he discovered a disquieting development: a company-wide meeting had been scheduled to address the precarious financial state of the organization.

The management presented two options; either reducing the workforce through attrition or eliminating non-essential departments altogether. Among them was Jonathan's department, where he had worked for some time. The realization later on that he was relieved of his duties only added to his already overwhelming emotional turmoil.

His affliction was augmented, swirling him into a pit of confusion. This upheaval immediately caused him distress, and without any income, everything would become unpredictable and more complicated. Jonathan's world seemed to crumble beneath him, leaving him stranded in a sea of uncertainty with no lifeline in sight.

On the other side, Tusoli's mom was doing all she could to bring her daughter back to her bubbly self. She was frustrated by Jonathan's actions that had left her daughter bedraggled. Tusoli's mother showered her with love and support, determined to help her through this tumultuous time. She cooked her favorite meals, took her out for walks in the park, and listened patiently as Tusoli poured out her heart. She even wrote her a letter to remind her how special she is.

Dear Daughter

You are not too much. You are simply too much for those accustomed to so little. You harbor a greatness so profound that it challenges their beliefs. You are a masterpiece, but it takes a true connoisseur to recognize your value.

In a world that often settles for mediocrity, your brilliance can be overwhelming to those who haven't dared to dream beyond the ordinary. Your ambitions, talents, and spirit shine with an intensity that can be intimidating, yet they are precisely what set you apart. It's not that you are too much; it's that the world sometimes lacks the capacity to embrace your full potential.

While some may see fault lines upon you, there is a light that emanates from within those faults, guiding those who truly see your value. They might count your mistakes, but the truth is you are made of greatness. Every perceived flaw is but a part of the intricate design that makes you extraordinary, illuminating the path for others who aspire to see beyond the surface.

What you are chasing, only a few have the courage to chase. Your dreams are not mere fantasies; they are the aspirations that define your journey. The road less traveled may seem daunting, but it is where you find the challenges that shape your character and lead to unparalleled fulfillment. Embrace the pursuit of your passions, knowing that in doing so, you inspire others to discover their own courage and chase their dreams alongside you.

Days turned into weeks, and weeks turned into months, yet Jonathan's efforts to win Tusoli back seemed futile. She remained steadfast in her decision to cut all ties with him. The pain of betrayal had left a deep wound, and she wasn't ready to forgive him just yet. However, amidst the tumult of emotions that engulfed her, she couldn't help but wonder if there was a possibility of salvaging their relationship.

Jonathan, too, grappled with his own turmoil. He was consumed by remorse and regret for his actions, and he knew he had caused irreparable damage to their relationship. Despite his efforts to make amends and prove his sincerity, Tusoli's heart remained closed to him. But whether they would ever find their way back to each other remained uncertain.. fate had a way of intervening.

Four months later, while in Auburn, Tusoli bumped into Pete, an old acquaintance from college. Pete had been there for her during the difficult time of her breakup with Jonathan, providing a shoulder to cry on and words of comfort when she needed them most. Little did Tusoli know that Pete had always harbored a deep, secret love for her, long before she even met Jonathan back in college. He had always seen her as a mystery, someone he couldn't help but be drawn to. However, he was never brave enough to confess his feelings to her, and before he knew it, she was already in a relationship with Jonathan. But even then, he never stopped loving her, and seeing her heartbroken and vulnerable reignited the feelings he had kept hidden for so long. His emotions would eventually burst forth into poetry.

You are a mystery
Love at first sight
That's what it was for me
The poetic beauty in your eyes
It's your large views of Life.
I learned to love you just as I love the sea
Yet it harbors so much that I can't even see
You dwell in my memory
Please save me from this agony.
For you I will throw heart and soul
Even though the novelty of being in love wore me off.
I wait in the summer and in winter fall
The most I can do is draw your Sketches and play golf.
We could carry on a surreptitious affair
Maybe you can escape him for new air
His depressing conditions and not so merry life
Come to me and I will make You my wife.
I did a small painting executed by my pencil
Just to bring out my view of who you are
That vigorous and masterful spirit
That shines bright even from far.
Trapped in an inauspicious beginning and complex entanglement,
Yet you are a rare piece of Jewel,
a renewed piece of intimacy, a fortress of moral rectitude.
Standing here on the margins of this raging rivers,
Am trying to catch the echo of your avenging artillery.
You were too timid to ask for what you wanted
But now Majestic and invincible
You came out of periods of dark depression
An imperturbable tranquility.
You are a Mystery.

THE BURIAL

The weight of grief hung heavily in the air in Africatown. The community mourned the loss of one of their brightest stars, a young woman with boundless dreams and an infectious spirit. But today, instead of celebrating her accomplishments and potential, they gathered to say their final goodbyes. The streets were lined with mourners, their faces etched with sorrow as they paid their respects to a life gone too soon. The church bells tolled solemnly, echoing the somber mood that enveloped the town. As they laid her to rest, the heavens wept with them, as if mourning the loss of a soul taken too soon.

Love me to Death
Love is not a fist,
Or a slap, or a shove,
It's not a hurtful word,
Or a threat with a glove.
Love is not control,
Or a power trip,
It's not about domination,
Or making your partner slip.
Love is respect,
And understanding too,
It's kindness and care,
And making their dreams come true.
Love is a safe place,
Where one can be themselves,
It's a haven from the world,
A sanctuary where peace dwells.
So, let's stand up to violence,
And say no to abuse,
Let's make love the center,
And let it be our refuge.
For every woman and every man,
Deserves to be treated with love,
So, let's speak out and act,
And make a world where love is enough.

She was more than just a friend to many; she was a daughter, a confidante. Her passion for life was palpable, and her hunger for success was insatiable. But her heart was captured by someone who didn't deserve her love, a cruel and callous man who extinguished her light. The tragedy of her death was almost too much to bear. Her absence left a void in the hearts of all who knew her, a void that could never truly be filled. The pain of losing her was a heavy burden to carry, and though she may be gone, her spirit would live on in the memories of those whose lives she touched.

Two weeks earlier, she was rushed to the emergency room, the victim of what is believed to have been a horrific act of domestic violence. A few months had passed since they rekindled their relationship and began living together. Jonathan had found a new job, and they decided to start afresh, especially since Karina was pregnant with his child. However, in the days leading up to their fresh start, Jonathan made every effort to win back Tusoli's heart. He showered her with apologies, promises, and gestures of love, hoping to erase the pain he had caused. Regardless of his words or actions, she remained resolute in her decision to never get back with him.

Karina carried Jonathan's baby for almost four more months after the failed termination attempt. Jonathan, realizing Tusoli was never getting back with him, rekindled his relationship with Karina, perhaps out of a sense of obligation to their child. As if to make Tusoli envious and worried that he might have been replaced in her life, he made his relationship with Karina seem perfect. Although Karina's father, Rudolph, strongly opposed this relationship with Jonathan, in the end, Karina couldn't really be stopped. On impulse, without premeditation, she abrogated her studies and moved in with him. Karina and Jonathan continued living together until the sixth month of her pregnancy when she tragically had an unexpected miscarriage.

The loss of their child weighed heavily on her, and it caused a sudden shift in Jonathan's behavior. He became increasingly violent, lashing out at Karina with unfathomable rage. Despite this, Karina stayed with him, her love blinding her to the danger that lurked behind his actions. But even her steadfast devotion could not quell the rising tide of Jonathan's frustration; if anything, it seemed to intensify it. As the cracks in their relationship deepened, Jonathan sought solace in the arms of other women, his infidelity a painful betrayal that cut deep into Karina's already wounded heart. It became painfully clear that his anger and resentment were not merely directed at Karina, but were rooted in the ashes of the failed relationship with Tusoli—a ghost that haunted their every interaction.

Yet, amidst the chaos, Karina clung to the fragile hope that Jonathan's heart would eventually find its way back to her. She believed that if she loved him enough, if she stood by him through the darkest of times, he would realize that she was the one who truly cared for him. But as the cycle of violence and infidelity continued, it became increasingly evident that Jonathan's demons ran far deeper than she could ever have imagined. And with each passing day, Karina found herself slipping further into the abyss of his tumultuous world, her own sense of self-worth eroded by the toxic whirlwind of their relationship.

After days of wrestling with her thoughts and emotions, Karina reached a breaking point. With a heavy heart and trembling hands, she dialed her mother's number, the weight of her decision pressing down on her like a suffocating blanket. As her mother's voice filled the line, Karina struggled to find the words to express the turmoil raging inside her. Finally, in a shaky voice, she confessed her desire to escape the suffocating grip of her tumultuous relationship with Jonathan. Tears streamed down her cheeks as she poured out her heart, sharing the pain and fear that had consumed her in recent months. All she wanted was to return to the safety and comfort of her childhood home, to escape the toxic cycle of violence and betrayal that had become her reality. She knew it wouldn't be easy, but she couldn't bear the thought of spending another day trapped in a relationship that was slowly destroying her.

But fate had other plans, cruel and unforgiving in its timing. In a moment of desperation, just when Jonathan entered the shower, Karina seized his phone, her fingers trembling as she scrolled through the damning evidence of Jonathan's infidelity. Her heart raced with a mixture of anger, betrayal and despair. With each incriminating message and photo, her fury intensified, fueled by the raw pain of his deceit.

With a surge of adrenaline coursing through her veins, Karina's anger ignited like a flame in the darkness, consuming her rationality in its fervent blaze. Without a second thought, she burst into the bathroom, her eyes blazing with righteous indignation. She confronted Jonathan head-on, her voice trembling with emotion as she hurled accusations at him. But Jonathan's response was not one of remorse or contrition. Instead, he erupted in a violent frenzy, his pent-up rage boiling over like a volcano.

With a savage primal roar of rage, he lashed out, his hands connecting with Karina's body with brutal force. She staggered backward and in a split second of terror, she felt herself hurtling towards the sharp edge of the marble sink right in front of her, her body colliding with the unyielding surface with a sickening thud. Pain exploded through her senses, white-hot and all-consuming, as darkness swallowed her whole.

The sickening crack of impact filled the room as Karina's world spun into total darkness, her consciousness slipping away like grains of sand through clenched fists. Blood trickled from the gash on her forehead, mingling with the tears that streamed down her cheeks. Every breath was a struggle, each heartbeat a painful reminder of the betrayal she had endured. Lying crumpled on the cold bathroom floor, Karina's mind teetered on the edge of consciousness, her vision clouded by darkness. In that moment she felt utterly alone, abandoned by the one person she had trusted the most in the world.

In a frantic blur of panic and desperation, Jonathan, realizing the severity of the situation, scooped Karina into his arms and rushed her to the nearest hospital where she was taken to the emergency room. He watched helplessly as a team of medical professionals swarmed around Karina, their urgent movements depicting the severity of her condition. Jonathan's voice shook as he addressed one of the emergency responders, "Please, you have to help her. She's not responding."

The responder nodded grimly, "We're doing everything we can. Hang in there."

As Karina was rushed into the theater, Jonathan paced anxiously in the waiting area, his mind swirling with a whirlwind of guilt and fear. He prayed silently for Karina's recovery, knowing deep down that he was responsible for the tragedy that had unfolded.

Inside the operating room, the doctors worked tirelessly to stabilize Karina's condition. The head surgeon conferred with the nurses, his voice urgent and determined, "We need to get her into surgery right away. We can't waste any time."As they prepared for the operation, another doctor approached Jonathan, his expression grave.

"Sir, I need to ask you some questions about what happened. Can you tell me how she sustained these injuries?"

Jonathan's throat felt dry as he recounted the events that had led to Karina's condition, his voice trembling with emotion. "We had an argument, and she fell... I didn't mean for this to happen."

The doctor nodded solemnly, jotting down notes on his clipboard. "Thank you for your cooperation. We'll do everything we can for her."

With each passing moment, Karina's life slipped further and further away, hours passed like an eternity as Jonathan waited anxiously for any news. Finally, the surgeon emerged from the operating room, his face weary but determined. "We did everything we could, but I'm sorry... Karina didn't make it," he said, his voice heavy with sorrow. Jonathan's world shattered as the reality of the situation sank in. Karina was gone, her light extinguished in a cruel twist of fate, and Jonathan was left to grapple with the consequences of his actions.

Mr. Rudolph was struck with immense grief upon learning about his daughter's untimely demise. He couldn't help but recall all the warnings he had given her about Jonathan, urging her to stay away from him especially after what had occurred with Tusoli. Now, those warnings felt like cruel echoes of a past he could never reclaim. Tears streamed down Mr. Rudolph's weathered face as he clutched a framed photograph of Karina, his fingers trembling with anguish. He wished he could turn back time, to rewrite the script of their lives and spare his daughter from the pain and suffering she had gone through. The agony of losing Karina was almost unbearable, a gaping wound in his heart that would never fully heal. He found himself haunted by the specter of what could have been, tormented by the cruel twist of fate that had robbed him of his precious daughter. In the silence of his grief-stricken solitude, Mr. Rudolph wept for the loss of a life cut tragically short, and for the shattered dreams that would never come to fruition.

Tusoli's heart sank as she received the news of Karina's passing. Shock and disbelief washed over her, leaving her numb and speechless. Karina was more than just a friend; she was a sister, a confidante, someone who had been by her side through thick and thin since their childhood. She couldn't help but think back to all the memories they had shared, the laughter and tears, the late-night conversations and the moments of joy. Despite the pain they had both endured at the hands of Jonathan, Tusoli had never blamed Karina. She knew that Karina was a victim too, caught in the web of Jonathan's deceit and manipulation. Now, as she grappled with the reality of Karina's passing, Tusoli felt a deep sense of loss. The world seemed colder and darker without her friend in it. She wished she could turn back time, to tell Karina how much she meant to her, how grateful she was for their friendship. But now, all she could do was mourn the loss of someone who had been a constant presence in her life, someone who had always stood by her side.

Today was a day filled with indescribable sadness as Tusoli joined family and friends to bid her final farewell to her best friend Karina. Amidst a sea of mourners, She stood defiantly, shaking her head, her heart heavy with grief as she watched Karina's casket being lowered into the ground. It felt like the world had come to a standstill, as if time itself had frozen for her. She couldn't bring herself to accept that her best friend was gone, that she would never hear her laughter or feel her comforting presence again. Tears streamed down Tusoli's cheeks, mingling with the raindrops that fell from the gray sky above as she realized that this was Karina's final journey, a journey from which there would be no return, and there was nothing she could do to bring her back. Each tear drop felt like a silent lament, a mournful chorus echoing the collective sorrow of all who had gathered to say their final goodbyes.

The weight of the pain Tusoli felt was unbearable, and it seemed like the world had stopped spinning just for her. She couldn't comprehend how someone so full of life could be gone forever, leaving nothing behind but the memory of her beautiful spirit. It was an inexorable grief that consumed her, and she could only hope that justice would be served, and Jonathan would be punished for the cruel and heartless act that took Karina's life.

Following the emotional burial that evening, Tusoli and Helena joined the grieving Rudolph family at their home to honor Karina's life. They shared memories and stories of her, by recalling her unwavering strength, her fearless spirit, and her remarkable determination. They spoke of her infectious charm, her quick wit, and her graceful demeanor, as well as her passion for art, languages, and literature. Helena, with tears glistening in her eyes, recounted fond memories of Karina's visits to their home, her laughter filling the room with joy. She spoke of Karina's love for cooking, her knack for storytelling, and her genuine kindness towards others. It was a solemn and bittersweet gathering, marked by both tears and laughter, as they celebrated the life of a beloved daughter and confidant.

After the somber gathering, Tusoli and her mother walked back to their house just a few yards away from the Rudolphs.

"Tusoli, I just want you to know how much I admire your strength and resilience. You've been through so much in the past year – the drama with Jonathan, the loss of your grandfather, and now losing your best friend Karina," Helena said, her words laced with empathy.

Tusoli looked at her mother with tears streaming down her face. "It's just been so hard, Mama. I don't know how to make sense of it all. Why did Karina have to die like that?" Her voice trembled with emotion as she spoke.

Helena listened, her heart breaking for her daughter. "I know, sweetheart. It's incredibly unfair," she replied softly, her own eyes misting with tears.

"Grandpa lived a full life, and we were able to say goodbye to him with love and gratitude. But Karina... it's just not fair. She was so young, with so much potential and so much to live for. And to have her life stolen from her in such a brutal manner, it's just unbearable." Tusole cried, her voice choked with grief. "All she did was love him, and for that she paid the ultimate price." she spoke painfully.

Helena put her hand on Tusoli's shoulder, feeling the weight of her words. "It's okay to feel angry and hurt, Tusoli. Karina's death was a tragedy and no one deserves to go through what she went through. We'll make sure that justice is served for what happened to her."

In the aftermath of Karina's tragic death, Tusoli was angry. Angry at Jonathan for his callous actions, angry at herself for not seeing the signs sooner, angry at the world for allowing such tragedy to occur. She vowed to fight for justice, to ensure that Karina's death would not go unpunished.

Thereafter, Tusoli was propelled by an unyielding determination to stand against domestic violence. Seeing parallels between it and historical slavery, she viewed it as a stripping away of fundamental rights. She embarked on a mission to raise awareness, organizing rallies, speaking at conferences, and sharing Karina's story. But she didn't stop there; she also collaborated with local organizations to develop programs offering counseling, legal aid, and job training for victims. With unwavering commitment, Tusoli fought for a world where women could break free from the chains of abuse and oppression. Her efforts inspired others to join her in the fight for justice and equality.

CHAPTER 10
THE JOURNEY TO AFRICA

After everything that Tusoli went through, especially losing her friend Karina, her desire to journey to Africa burned even brighter.

Helena had long anticipated the arrival of this day; it loomed in the horizon like inevitable fate. Her daughter, Tusoli, possessed a deep thirst for knowledge and an unwavering commitment to unravel the enigma of their family lineage. Ever since Helena regaled her daughter with the stories of slavery that had been passed down through their family, Tusoli had been on an engrossing journey of self-discovery. The discovery of The Clotilda was a pivotal moment that further ignited her quest. She was eager to follow its trail back in time, to where it all began and ended. Tusoli found herself drawn inexorably to the land from whence her ancestors were forcibly taken. It was more than just a journey; it was a pilgrimage—a quest to reclaim a piece of her heritage and to honor the resilience of those who came before her.

Tusoli's longing to visit Africa was so intense that she made the bold decision to resign from her job in Auburn. Her heart was set on exploring the slave caves in Kenya, to immerse herself in the local communities and hear their narratives surrounding the harrowing legacy of the slave trade. Her grandfather had been a staunch supporter of her expedition, and he had even made provisions for her in his will. Upon his passing, a substantial inheritance from his extensive estate would be transferred into Tusoli's bank account, providing the financial means for Tusoli to embark on her journey. With her mother settled in Auburn and her bakery business up and running, Tusoli focused all her energy on finalizing arrangements for her long-awaited expedition. They made the decision to lease out their residence in Africatown following a thorough renovation. Seeing her mother enjoy her newfound entrepreneurial endeavor and embrace the life she rightfully deserved brought immense satisfaction to Tusoli's heart.

With everything in order, Tusoli stood on the brink of commencing her odyssey. Her itinerary outlined a stop in New York before ultimately setting course for Africa, where she longed to trace the footsteps of Abisai and the countless other enslaved souls who had etched their history into the fabric of the black community in Africatown, her cherished birthplace and hometown.

Tusoli savored the warm and joyful evening with her mother, basking in their loving connection over a delectable meal. They indulged in a glass of exquisite wine at a quaint restaurant nestled within the heart of the city—a poignant farewell repast, marking their final soirée together before Tusoli embarked on her journey the next day.

Drenched in excitement and anticipation, Tusoli stood poised with her belongings meticulously packed ready for the impending adventure. As the clock struck 7 in the morning, Pete arrived in his sleek and lustrous black Mercedes sedan, the vehicle purring softly as it pulled up to the curb. With deft efficiency, he helped Tusoli load her bags and travel essentials into the capacious trunk. With a final glance at her childhood home, Tusoli took a deep breath, feeling the weight of her journey ahead. Together, they embarked on the road to the airport, the gateway to her dreams awaiting beyond the horizon.

They reached Jackson Airport in Atlanta, Georgia where they had their last reflective moments before Tusoli's flight to New York which was scheduled at 11am that day. With her heart aflutter, she gazed out of the expansive window, captivated by the choreography of planes ascending and descending against the canvas of the clear blue sky. Feeling as if she was on the cusp of an adventure that would change her life forever, Tusoli turned to her mother, "Mom, I can barely believe it's truly unfolding," Tusoli murmured, reaching out to clasp her mother's hand in a tender embrace.

Helena smiled at her daughter, her eyes shining with pride. "You're following your dreams, my dear. I couldn't be more proud of the woman you've become"

Tusoli embraced her mother tightly, cherishing the comfort of her presence. "I owe it all to you, Mom. You've been my unwavering support."

Helena gently grasped her daughter's hands, her gaze filled with assurance. "You're ready for this, Tusoli. Carry with you all that I've taught you, and seize every moment of this expedition."

Tusoli nodded earnestly, her eyes shimmering with gratitude and determination. "I won't forget, Mom. I'll treasure every experience."

Pete's timely presence interrupted their tender moment, prompting Tusoli to turn towards him with a warm smile.

"Tusoli, I just want to say how proud I am of you for taking this journey. It takes a lot of courage to follow your dreams like this," Pete expressed warmly, his smile reflecting genuine admiration.

Tusoli reciprocated his smile, deeply touched by his support. "Thank you, Pete. Your encouragement means the world to me," she responded gratefully.

Pete then reached into his pocket and pulled out a small gift wrapped in a brown paper bag, "I also wanted to give you this," he said as he handed the gift to her.

Unwrapping the package, Tusoli was met with a gasp of awe at the sight of a beautiful bracelet crafted from intricate African beads. "It's truly stunning!" she exclaimed in astonishment.

"I acquired it on a recent excursion. I hoped it might serve as a talisman of sorts, guiding you on your journey," Pete explained with a warm sincerity.

Tusoli was touched by the gesture and carefully wore the bracelet on her wrist. "Thank you, Pete. I will treasure this," she expressed with a heartfelt smile.

Tusoli felt a pang of bittersweet emotion as the final call for her flight echoed through the airport terminal. She clung tightly to her mother and Pete who gave her a short kiss, both wishing her the best on her journey. With tear-filled eyes, she promised to stay in touch and return soon. She then took a deep breath and made her way towards the gate, casting one final glance over her shoulder, to see her loved ones waving goodbye. With a flutter of excitement and a whisper of apprehension, Tusoli ventured forth towards the threshold of her next grand adventure.

Pete watched Tusoli's figure disappear behind the gate, feeling both sadness and admiration for her bravery. He wished he could have told her how he truly felt about her, but he knew that it was not the time. He turned to Helena, placing a comforting hand on her shoulder.

"She'll be back before we know it," he said, trying to lift her spirits.

Helena nodded, wiping a tear from her cheek. "I know," she said, "but it's hard to let go of your child, especially when they're off to explore unknown lands."

Pete nodded in agreement, feeling deep empathy for Helena's worries.

"She's a strong woman," he told her, "and she's got your strength and resilience in her. She'll be alright."

Helena smiled, grateful for Pete's words of comfort. "Thank you, Pete," she replied, "for everything you've done for us. You've been a true friend and a pillar of support for Tusoli when she needed it most."

Pete smiled back at her. "It was the least I could do," he said, "you and Tusoli are like family to me. And speaking of family," he added, "how about we grab some breakfast? My treat."

Helena chuckled, feeling a bit of relief and gratitude for Pete's presence in her life. "Sounds like a plan," she said, "I could use a good cup of coffee right now."

With a heavy heart and a determined spirit, Tusoli boarded the plane, ready to rediscover her roots and the history of her ancestors in Africa.

As Pete and Helena departed from the airport, a heavy ache settled within his heart as he watched the airplane disappear into the sky. He had known Tusoli for years, their friendship growing stronger over time. But lately, he had begun to see her in a different light. Pete couldn't deny the burgeoning emotions that had begun to stir within him, a desire to be more than just friends with Tusoli.

As they walked away from the gate with her mother, Pete wondered if Tusoli had any inkling of his feelings. He had been careful not to give away anything, but perhaps there had been subtle hints that she had picked up on. Nevertheless, he remained steadfast in his decision to keep his affections veiled. The fear of losing Tusoli as a friend was too great, and he couldn't bear the thought of jeopardizing their bond over something as uncertain as romantic feelings. He hoped that Tusoli would return from her journey with a renewed sense of self and perhaps even some clarity about their relationship. Until then, he would keep his distance, and his heart would always yearn for her. For now, it's just goodbye.

Goodbye

An utterance of goodbye
A parting statement,
I have breathed a sigh,
Yield to my sentiment.
Am not afraid you are going
My heart says you may not return
I will wait in bleak rustling
In freezing moon or blazing sun.
To love you means to acquiesce
That the ride will only last a while
What will matter is you said Yes
I grappled with life to make you smile.
I hope you will conquer your demon,
Am no promise of perfect tranquility
Neither not in the shape of a hellion
But a picture of elegance and serenity.
If you don't get to come back to me
Then this is the last I see of you
He will be lucky whoever it will be
You've been my rainbow in the hue.
A kiss is one I would beg
At least for I know it will stay
That'll take me down a peg!
There's so much I could say.
But for now, it's Goodbye!

Tusoli sat on the plane lost in her thoughts, unexpectedly reminded of the short but sweet kiss that Pete had given her at the airport lounge. This simple gesture stirred a cascade of emotions and brought back a flood of memories, including the bittersweet recollection of Jonathan, the first person who had ever kissed her. She remembered the day he surprised her with a band singing *'Clotilde is on fire'*, and the night he proposed to her under the starry sky in Auburn. These memories held a special place in her heart, and she knew they always would. Despite the heartbreak that had followed, she could not deny the joy and love that had once filled her life. Yet, amidst the nostalgia, Tusoli couldn't help but ponder the fate of Jonathan, now incarcerated. Despite the pain he had caused, a pang of compassion tugged at her heartstrings as she envisioned the hardships he was likely enduring behind bars. Despite the complexities of their past, Tusoli found herself unable to fully extinguish the ember of empathy that flickered within her.

This surge of memories triggered a mix of poignant feelings, reminding her of the love she had lost and the heartache she had endured. Though she felt a twinge of pain, Tusoli hoped her pilgrimage to Africa held the promise not only of rediscovering her ancestral heritage but also of embarking on a journey of personal healing and renewal. Two years later, Tusoli finds herself reflecting on the transformative journey she embarked upon, she ponders whether she is finally prepared to embrace the prospect of moving on and the myriad possibilities that lay ahead.

As the plane began its descent towards LaGuardia airport in New York, Tusoli shook herself out of her reverie, ready to face the new chapter of her life that awaited her. When the plane finally came to a halt and the passengers were allowed to disembark, Tusoli felt a mix of excitement and apprehension.

"We've finally arrived in New York," the passenger next to her exclaimed.

"Yeah, it was a quick flight," Tusoli responded absentmindedly, her thoughts still elsewhere.

"I'm Leo. We didn't get a chance to talk much. You seemed a bit preoccupied," Leo remarked.

"I'm Tusoli. I didn't even realize it until now," Tusoli replied, offering a small smile.

They left the airplane, and Tusoli grabbed her luggage before hailing a taxi to her hotel in New York.

CHAPTER 11
NEW YORK CITY

The warm rays of the early morning sun peered through the windows of Tusoli's hotel room in New York City, gently awakening her. With five more nights to spend in the city before her scheduled flight to Africa, she planned to make the most of her time by visiting various slave museums in New York to delve deeper into its history and culture, particularly the legacy of slavery and Black heritage.

In addition, she had made plans to explore local restaurants, businesses, and other attractions in the city. Tusoli was determined to soak up all the experiences the city had to offer and make this trip a memorable one. She was excited to delve deeper into the rich history of New York City, having learned that it was once the capital of American slavery for more than two centuries. She felt a sense of urgency to explore the city's historical treasures and learn more about the struggles and triumphs of Black culture throughout the years.

She started her day on Wall Street, between Pearl and Water Streets, where a market once auctioned enslaved people of African ancestry. With the help of a local guide, she visited the famous African Burial Ground National Monument, which to date, contains the remains of more than 419 free and enslaved Africans buried during the late 17th and 18th centuries. John greeted her warmly and began to explain the significance of the site.

"Good morning, Tusoli. I'm glad you made it. This is the African Burial Ground National Monument. It contains the remains of more than 419 free and enslaved Africans buried during the late 17th and 18th centuries," John said.

"Wow, that's incredible," Tusoli replied. "I had no idea that there were so many Africans buried here."

"Yes, this is just one of many historical sites in the city that tell the story of the African-American experience. This site was actually rediscovered in 1991 during the construction of a federal office building. The remains were carefully excavated and examined, revealing a wealth of information about the lives of enslaved Africans in New York City and it was later designated as a National Monument in 2006," John continued.

Tusoli nodded, impressed by the rich history that surrounded her. "What else do you have planned for our tour today?" she asked.

"Well, next we're going to visit the African American Museum in Harlem, where you can learn more about the history of African Americans in New York City," John replied.

"I'm looking forward to it," Tusoli said with a smile.

Tusoli visited several other sites related to Black history in New York City, including the Schomburg Center for Research in Black Culture and the Harlem Renaissance Museum. She ended her day with a meal at *Sylvia's Soul Food* in Harlem, which has been serving traditional Southern cuisine since the 1960s, savoring the flavors and spices that had been passed down through generations of Black Americans. She also visited Black-owned *Brooklyn Tea* in Bed-Stuy, which offers a variety of teas and baked goods.

During her tour, she learned about the underground railroad, a network of abolitionists who helped nearly 100,000 runaway slaves escape the arduous, lonely labor and offered them shelter, food, and finally a way out to free states. Tusoli was captivated by the stories of the brave men and women who risked their lives to help slaves find their freedom through the Underground Railroad. She visited the Harriet Tubman Home, where she learned about the life of this iconic abolitionist who led many slaves to freedom. The Frederick Douglass Memorial and Historical Association was another stop on her itinerary, commemorating the life and legacy of another famous abolitionist. She listened intently as the guide recounted the struggles and triumphs of these remarkable individuals, feeling a deep sense of admiration for their courage and determination.

As she walked through the city, she couldn't help but feel the weight of history on her shoulders. She wondered what it must have been like to be a slave in a bustling metropolis like New York, where human beings were bought and sold like commodities. She was grateful for the opportunity to learn about this dark period in American history, but she was also hopeful that by understanding the past, she could help shape a better future.

Despite its name, the Underground Railroad wasn't an actual railroad as one might imagine. It was a network of secret routes and safe houses established during the 19th century to help enslaved African Americans escape to free states and Canada. The term "railroad" was used metaphorically, with "conductors" guiding runaway slaves from one safe house or station to the next. These conductors included liberated slaves and brave abolitionists, both White and Black, who risked their lives to help others find freedom. Each safe house and station along the route formed a crucial link in the Underground Railroad, providing shelter, food, and guidance to those seeking a path to liberty.

Tusoli had the opportunity to travel the paths taken by freedom seekers and visit landmarks that make up the Underground Railroad, celebrating the history and heroes that guided them to freedom. She discovered a vast network of churches, safe houses, and community sites in New York, as well as the 445-mile border with Canada, which were used to help emancipate enslaved people. Throughout her stay in New York, Tusoli explored the stories of America's bravest abolitionists who played a vital role in shaping the state's history on slavery, ultimately leading to the final ban on the slave trade.

She visited various sites such as The Harriet Tubman National Historic Park, the North Star Underground Railroad Museum, the Niagara Falls Underground Railroad Heritage Center, the John W. Jones Museum, and many more. These landmarks provided her with a deeper understanding of the struggles and victories of the abolitionists who fought tirelessly for the freedom of enslaved people. She immersed herself in the stories and exhibits, feeling a profound sense of connection to the courageous individuals who risked their lives to help others find freedom.

During her visit to Niagara Falls, Tusoli explored the Underground Railroad Heritage Area and gained a deeper understanding of the local history surrounding the abolitionist movement and the Underground Railroad. She listened to guided tours and examined exhibits that highlighted the struggles and triumphs of freedom seekers who passed through the area on their journey to freedom.

Tusoli also delved into the African American history collection at The New York State Museum, which housed a vast collection of documents related to slavery in the state, the efforts to abolish it, military accomplishments, civil rights activities, and the daily lives of African Americans living in New York State. She was captivated by the stories of resilience and perseverance, finding inspiration in individuals like Harriet Tubman, whose courage and determination fueled her own quest to follow the path taken by her ancestors to Africatown.

Tubman, a brave abolitionist, not only liberated herself but also returned to Maryland about thirteen times to rescue friends and family from the chains of slavery. Her contributions helped shape the underground railroad network, which is a significant part of African American history and is believed to have helped more than 100,000 slaves find their freedom. Tusoli greatly admired Tubman's strength, valor, and humanity.

In her own words, Tubman said, "I was the conductor of the Underground Railroad for eight years, and I can say what most conductors can't say — I never ran my train off the track and I never lost a passenger." – Harriet Tubman at a suffrage convention, New York, 1896.

Tubman's words were a testament to her commitment and bravery in helping enslaved people escape to freedom. Her success in guiding countless individuals through the Underground Railroad was a remarkable achievement and a reminder of the courage and resilience of those who fought against slavery. Her words continue to inspire and empower people today.

Tusoli was deeply inspired by Harriet Tubman's story and decided to follow her path in the underground railroad network. She felt a strong connection to Tubman's determination and resolve, and she was determined to honor her legacy by retracing the steps of freedom seekers and continuing the fight for justice and equality.

Tusoli's journey began with a visit to the Harriet Tubman Underground Railroad Visitor Center, situated in Church Creek, Maryland, where Tubman's acts of resistance began. The center, nestled in a coastal and marshy environment, comprises two front gable buildings on the second story. Inside, a permanent exhibit provides a detailed description of Tubman's legacy, while other exhibits focus on the Underground Railroad experiences from a regional perspective.

Continuing her exploration, Tusoli visited the Tubman-Garrett Riverfront Park and sculpture, which commemorates the bond of trust and friendship between Harriet Tubman and other abolitionists, such as Quaker Thomas Garrett. The sculpture celebrates their critical collaborations between 1854 and 1860.

Further along the Underground Railroad network, Tusoli arrived at the William Still Marker located at 244 S. 12th Street in Philadelphia. William Still, a prominent abolitionist, dedicated himself to aiding freedom seekers who had liberated themselves. He lived in a home near this marker and wrote and published "The Underground Railroad," a book that chronicles the stories of the people he assisted on their journey to freedom. This book remains an influential work in shaping our understanding of the Underground Railroad today.

Tusoli savored the serene ambiance of the Beach Boardwalk at South Cape May Meadows. This picturesque location held significant historical importance for freedom seekers who sought independence in Cape May, New Jersey, after braving the treacherous waters of the Delaware Bay. As she strolled along the boardwalk, Tusoli reflected on the contrast between the pro-slavery states of Virginia and Delaware and the anti-slavery state of New Jersey, symbolizing the ongoing struggle for equality.

Continuing her journey, Tusoli arrived at The Stephen and Harriet Myers Residence, a historic landmark in Albany, New York. This residence served as a vital hub for Underground Railroad activity. The Myers, prominent Black Abolitionists, hosted meetings of the Albany Vigilance Committee, an organization dedicated to assisting freedom seekers, at their home throughout the 1850s. Additionally, the Myers provided shelter to individuals on the Underground Railroad, offering them safety and support on their journey to freedom.

During her journey, Tusoli made a significant stop at the Gerrit Smith Estate, where she delved into the life of Gerrit Smith, a prominent abolitionist whose contributions were instrumental in New York's abolition movement. Today, the Gerrit Smith Estate is recognized as a site on the Network to Freedom and holds the status of a National Historic Landmark. Spanning seven acres, the estate features exterior exhibits highlighting the Smiths, Black Americans, and the Underground Railroad. Visitors have the opportunity to explore four intact estate buildings, gaining insight into the history and significance of the abolitionist movement in New York.

Afterwards, Tusoli returned to the Niagara Falls Underground Railroad Heritage Center, an immersive museum dedicated to uncovering the true narratives of Underground Railroad escapees and abolitionists in Niagara Falls. Through interactive exhibits, the center encourages visitors to confront contemporary injustices stemming from slavery and to take action towards creating a more just society.

At the Combahee River Ferry, marked by the Harriet Tubman Memorial Bridge, Tusoli learned about the historic Combahee River Raid. In June 1863, Harriet Tubman and African American soldiers from the 2nd South Carolina Volunteer Infantry conducted this raid, freeing over 750 enslaved people.

Concluding her journey, Tusoli visited Harriet Tubman's home in Auburn, New York. Tubman had purchased a 7-acre plot of land there in 1859, where she lived and continued her abolitionist work. Tusoli then wrapped up her tour of the Underground Railroad network at the Thompson Memorial African Methodist Episcopal Zion Church, built in 1891. This church held significant importance to Tubman's community, serving as a place of worship for her and her family. Tubman's final resting place is located at the church, where she was buried after her death in 1913.

CHAPTER 12
NAIROBI KENYA

Tusoli's journey to New York had been enlightening, but her expedition to Kenya held even greater personal significance. It was a journey of self-discovery and a quest to connect with her African roots on a profound level. With anticipation coursing through her veins, Tusoli settled into her first-class seat aboard an Emirates flight from JFK airport to Nairobi.

The hours passed in a blur of anticipation and reflection. From the urban sprawl of New York to the vast expanse of the African landscape, Tusoli watched the world below transition. As they began their descent into Kenyan airspace, she pressed her face against the window, captivated by the breathtaking scenery below. The verdant landscape, dotted with small villages and meandering rivers, filled her with a sense of belonging she had never felt before.

Touching down at Jomo Kenyatta International Airport in Nairobi, Tusoli felt a surge of emotion. This was the beginning of a journey that would redefine her sense of identity and purpose, and she was ready to embrace every moment of it. The landing was smooth, and the airport bustled with activity as passengers disembarked and made their way through immigration and customs. Tusoli took a deep breath and stepped out into the warm African air, ready to begin her journey. After settling in at Sarova Stanley, Tusoli spent the first day exploring Nairobi's bustling streets. She visited museums and galleries like the Nairobi Archives, immersing herself in the rich history and culture of the city. Tusoli also indulged in sampling local cuisine, savoring the flavors and aromas of traditional Kenyan dishes. From spicy samosas to savory nyama choma, each bite was a culinary adventure.

In the course of her brief sojourn in Nairobi, Tusoli wasted no time immersing herself in the city's diverse and captivating culture. Her exploratory forays led her to an intriguing discovery: Nairobi boasts the distinction of being the only city in the world to harbor a National Park right on its doorstep. This verdant expanse encompasses a whopping 78,000 acres and teems with a thriving wildlife population, including a successful Rhinoceros sanctuary. Tusoli couldn't help but marvel at the breathtaking panorama of Nairobi's skyscrapers juxtaposed with the rare sight of these wild animals frolicking in their natural habitat at the park.

On the third day of her adventure, Tusoli was picked by a tour van from Akothee Safaris, ready to whisk her away on a journey to the west of Nairobi. Their destination: Narok County, nestled along the Great Rift Valley, a six-hour drive ahead.

They traversed the rugged terrain, and Tusoli found herself utterly mesmerized by the awe-inspiring landscape unfolding before her eyes. Towering hills and imposing cliffs dotted the horizon, remnants of the ancient forces that had shaped the Great Rift fault line over millennia. Each twist and turn of the road revealed a new vista, each more breathtaking than the last.

Narok County's crown jewel awaited them at journey's end—the renowned Masai Mara National Park. Home to a rich diversity of wildlife and boasting unparalleled natural beauty, the park promised an unforgettable experience for Tusoli and the chance to witness nature in all its unbridled glory.

Upon reaching the entrance of the *Masai Mara National Park*, Tusoli was instantly captivated by the boundless expanse and breathtaking beauty that stretched before her, a unique haven for spectacular wildlife diversity.

One of the world's *Seven Wonders,* the *great wildebeest migration*, occurs here every year between July and October, an awe-inspiring phenomenon that draws tourists and wildlife enthusiasts from every corner of the globe, offering a glimpse into the untamed beauty and raw power of the natural world.

The *Masai Mara National Park* and Tanzania's *Serengeti* are distinct from each other by *the Mara River,* which not only separates the two parks but also marks the transition of seasons. The wildebeests are compelled to migrate due to the uneven distribution of resources. They must traverse the treacherous waters of the mara river, teeming with ferocious crocodiles, to reach the greener pastures on either side. This natural barrier, the mara river, plays a pivotal role in shaping the lives of the wildebeests. The price they pay for their search for sustenance is what comprises a remarkable natural phenomenon, famously known as the Great Wildebeest Migration; a spectacle that has captured the imaginations of wildlife enthusiasts around the world.

Tusoli arrived at the serene and shaded stretch of the riverbank, thoughtfully arranged for her by the highly acclaimed Ker and Downey Safaris, the longest-running safari outfitter in Africa. She had impeccable timing, as she was just in time to witness one of the most magnificent spectacles of nature.

Over a million wildebeests would soon cross the treacherous Mara River from Tanzania's *Serengeti Reserve*, and Tusoli was about to witness a spectacle of nature unlike any other. She was mesmerized by the immense and enthralling spectacle as the wildebeests began to gather at the steep banks of the Mara River, stretching for miles like a trail of ants. Their lustrous coats and the billowing dust cloud from the valley below were visible from miles away. The clamor of their moans and explosive snorts filled the air of the Mara. She had never witnessed anything quite like it before. Amidst the swirling currents of the Mara River, lurk ferocious crocodiles lying in wait, their jaws poised to snatch unsuspecting prey.

Tusoli felt great empathy for the wildebeests as she observed their behavior. The animals were hesitant to make the first move, and it was clear that they were aware of the danger that lay ahead. The turbid waters and the hungry crocodiles were waiting. It was a reminder to her of how fear and uncertainty can affect even the most instinctual of creatures. After a long period of waiting and lowing, a single wildebeest finally emerged from the herd and summoned the courage to hurl itself off the steep riverbank and into the turbulent waters of the Mara River. Perhaps it was due to the collective force of the herd behind it, or perhaps it simply possessed an indomitable will to liberate the rest. Regardless, soon after the initial leap, the rest of the herd followed suit, charging into the river in a frenzied mass akin to a rolling storm.

Heedless of the chaos unfolding around them, they fought to climb up the jagged rocks on the opposite bank, determined to make it across at any cost. Amidst the turmoil and tumult of the river crossing, tragedy struck with unforgiving force. Some of the wildebeests, their bodies weakened by exhaustion and fear, succumbed to the relentless pull of the currents, disappearing beneath the surface without a trace. Others, caught in the frenzied scramble to escape, found themselves trampled upon by their own kind, their desperate cries drowned out by the roar of the rushing waters.

The river was teeming with wildebeests, crossing in their thousands, and it was a formidable challenge to survive the journey across the cold waters with hundreds of crocodiles lurking nearby. But there was no turning back or stopping now. Sadly, many were swiftly dragged under by large crocodiles. With each stroke of their powerful jaws, these ancient predators claimed their prey, dragging unsuspecting victims under the surface to meet a fate shrouded in darkness.

Meanwhile, on the adjacent plain, distressed calves dashed along the edges of the herd, calling out for their lost mothers. It was a slaughter of wildebeests en masse, a massacre that must occur every year during this great migration. The crossing of the river was a brutal and deadly experience. This was the brutal reality of life on the African savannah.

Despite the danger and the casualties, the wildebeests persisted in their migration, driven by a primal instinct to survive and thrive. It was a harrowing ordeal, a test of survival, and as the waters of the Mara River ran red with the blood of the fallen, it stood as a solemn reminder of the sacrifices made by the wildebeests each year during their epic migration—a sacrifice that ensured the continuation of their species, even in the face of nature's most unforgiving challenges.

Tusoli couldn't help but admire their determination and tenacity, even in the face of such perilous odds. She realized that this was a testament to the resilience and strength of nature, and that it was a privilege to witness such a magnificent display of life in action. As she watched the wildebeests struggle and fight to reach the other side of the river, she thought of the *enslaved* people who risked everything to gain their freedom. It was not easy to start a rebellion, many perished, and fear was a constant companion. However, a few brave individuals took the first step, inspiring others to join them, and history was changed forever.

Tusoli saw a powerful parallel between the wildebeest migration and the history of slavery, with the river serving as a symbolic barrier between oppression and liberation. As she watched the wildebeest muster their courage to cross the river and face the deadly crocodiles, she thought of the brave slaves who risked everything to escape bondage and reach freedom. To her, it was a reminder that the fight for freedom is never easy, and often requires great sacrifice and courage. Just like the wildebeests, slaves had to face dangerous obstacles to reach freedom. They too had to take that first leap of courage to escape from the oppression that always lingered around them. The consequences of staying put were equally dire, as they would continue to suffer inhuman treatment and forced labor. The bravery of those who escaped paved the way for millions of others to follow, just like the wildebeests who eventually crossed the river to reach their greener pastures. She savored a sundowner on the riverbank at her camp, finding the experience to be gratifying and fulfilling. As nightfall arrived, the migration was still ongoing, with straggling members of the massive herd still scrambling to cross the turbid waters. The journey would not end until the last wildebeest crossed the mighty Mara river.

Soon enough, a dusky hue enveloped the Mara. Tusoli's ears were filled with the haunting sounds of the migration, still echoing in the distance. With bated breath, she pondered how many of the wildebeests would succeed in crossing the Mara River, and how many would become prey for the lurking predators. But despite the danger, the wildebeests would continue their relentless journey, driven by an innate instinct to reach the other side, no matter the cost.

When the daylight finally faded and the darkness of the night fully engulfed the Masai Mara wilderness, Tusoli's experience took on a whole new dimension with the assistance of the knowledgeable *Angama Mara* guides. They introduced her to the stunning and unique features of the Masai Mara night sky, which were not always visible in urban areas. She was treated to a night truly unforgettable where she observed the shape of the *Milky Way*, the visible manifestation of the billions of stars in our galaxy, and the dark lanes of dust that interrupt its light.

Her guide was able to show her a star whose light left on its journey to Earth in the year she was born. There's nothing quite like it. It was mind blowing for Tusoli. She learnt that the light from our Sun's nearest neighboring star takes more than four years to reach us so when we look at the night sky, we are not just looking out in space but also back in time. She watched from the *Angama lodge's deck* as the *International Space Station,* with its five astronauts, sailed overhead. Some guests joined them and after the satellite passed, Tusoli was treated to a short tour of the constellations.

THE MASAI MARA NIGHT sky from Angama lodge's deck (picture courtesy of Angama)

As Tusoli enjoyed the breathtaking view of the sky above the Mara, she heard a voice behind her exclaim, "Wow, I have never seen anything quite like this."

Turning around, she recognized a familiar face, "I remember you from the plane," Tusoli greeted him. "I didn't know you were coming to Africa."

"I'm Leo," he replied. "I came for a safari in Kenya and to witness the wildebeest migration."

Tusoli responded, "That's fascinating! I'm on safari too, but for a different reason. The Angama guides planned this night tour of the milky way for me, and it's been an awe-inspiring experience."

Curious, Leo asked, "What kind of safari are you on?"

Tusoli explained, "I'm here to follow my history. My ancestors were taken from this country and brought to the US as slaves 160 years ago, and I want to retrace their steps.

"Leo remarked, "What an interesting endeavor. I'm sure it's satisfying to be here."

Tusoli replied, "My heart is full, Leo. Watching the wildebeest migration has reminded me of the courage and struggle my ancestors faced to find freedom."

Leo shared, "My ancestors were slave owners in Georgia, Atlanta. If I could have lived during their time, I would have been among those who fought for abolition."

Tusoli asked, "So you would be an abolitionist?"

Leo replied, "I would save whoever I could, to the last one of them, from the gruesome bondage."

Tusoli said, "That's amazing to hear. So, you're Leo from Georgia?"

Leo confirmed, "I'm Leonardo from Atlanta, Georgia."

"I'm Tusoli Tolewa from Africatown, Alabama," Tusoli introduced herself. "This trip is my way of discovering Africa's incredible story and culture, and walking in the paths of my forefathers."

"Pleasure to meet you, Tusoli," Leo complimented her. "You're very beautiful."

Tusoli smiled graciously, then both marveled at the night sky.

"Look at this night sky, the whole Milky way is just right here above us." Leo marveled.

"It's breathtaking, right?" Tusoli remarked. "I can't describe it, the animals, the sky, the maasai culture, everything about this place is pure magic."

Leo agreed, "It's totally inundating. This is my first time in Africa, and I'm treated to this wonder."

Tusoli added a bit lost in thought, "There's something about the first time. You just can't forget it."

Leo chuckled, "Yeah, this will forever remain in my memory, and so will you."

Tusoli grinned, "White boy with sweet words, I won't be in a hurry to leave your memories."

Leo laughed and asked, "Well, what are you doing after this? There's a bar at my hotel."

Tusoli declined, "I'm a little wasted, will probably retreat to my camp and get some rest."

"We can have a conversation tomorrow and talk a little more?" Leo suggested.

"Sure, Leonardo," Tusoli agreed. "Have a good night."

"Good night, Tusoli," Leo bid her farewell.

Leonardo was struck by Cupid's arrow the moment his eyes met Tusoli's on the flight from Georgia. As they parted ways at the bustling airport in New York, he couldn't shake the feeling of regret for not asking for her contact. But destiny had a different plan in store for him, as she appeared right in front of him once again. He couldn't help but marvel at her beauty and mysterious aura.

Her beauty and enigmatic essence left him in awe, and he yearned to unravel the depths of this striking and alluring lady. *"What a beautiful stranger"* he thought to himself.

Beautiful Stranger
A beautiful stranger
Or maybe a lone ranger
A cosmos traveler
Or just a hopeful earth dweller
Blue or brown eyes
Am sure of beautiful thighs
What's with loving strangers?
Is it because they live in a future we don't know,
Or is it because we feel they are people we've once known,
After all everyone we've ever loved was once peculiar even though some are so
gone.
How does she smile
Maybe she did.
Is it as beautiful as mine?
What about her feet?
What's her favorite quote
What's her best book
Would she tattoo my name
On the back of her neck
Or she would shout 'what the heck'.
How deep is her soul
Is it as silent as the flight of an owl
Or is it chaos inside her mind
Or could she be that one of a kind?
What's the sound in her voice
Is she a poet or just a novice?
What's the taste in her lips
What's the color of the skin on her hips?
I want to know.
Oh Beautiful stranger.

THE AFRICAN FESTIVAL

Tusoli was filled with anticipation as she prepared for the African Festival that was taking place in the Nairobi metropolis. Her excitement was evident as she carefully selected her attire for the concert, opting for a vibrant African print dress that accentuated her curves and complemented her complexion. Her chic afro hairstyle was the perfect complement to her overall look, and she adorned herself with a beaded necklace and bracelet, completing her ensemble with a touch of elegance.

She stepped out of her hotel and onto the busy streets of the Nairobi night life, swept away by the lively atmosphere that surrounded her. The city was alive with the rhythmic sounds of music and the buzz of chatter from the enthusiastic festival-goers. Tusoli couldn't help but feel an overwhelming sense of energy and excitement as she made her way towards the festival.

The vibrant culture of Nairobi was calling out to her, and she was eager to fully immerse herself in it. She enjoyed trying the local cuisine, which included dishes such as nyama choma (roasted meat), ugali (a maize-based dish), mayai pasua(boiled egg dashed with raw tomato,chilli and onion) and pilau (spiced rice). She even had the chance to shop for souvenirs at the vibrant Maasai night Market, where local vendors sold a variety of handmade crafts and textiles.

Upon her arrival at the carnivore grounds, Tusoli was greeted by the irresistible aroma of sizzling meats and the lively beat of drums that echoed throughout the open-air venue. Her eyes were immediately drawn to the stage, which was adorned with an impressive display of musical instruments. She caught a glimpse of the silhouette of the Sauti Sol band members, bustling about backstage in preparation for their performance.

Tusoli found a spot near the stage and swayed to the beat of the opening act. The crowd around her was a mix of locals and tourists, all united by their love of African music and culture. As the night wore on, Tusoli could hardly contain her excitement for the much-anticipated performance by her music idols, *Sauti Sol*. With the stage lights blaring and the crowd cheering, the band started playing their chart-topping song-*"Live and Die in Afrika."*

Tusoli couldn't help but sing along, feeling every word of the lyrics in her soul as she swayed to the beat of the music. Her voice echoed among the thousands of fans, and for a moment, she felt as though she was one with the music and the crowd. The pulsating beat of the music stirred her soul. The words of the chorus echoed in her mind as she moved to the rhythm, feeling a sense of belonging and purpose. The lyrics spoke of ambition, freedom, and courage, qualities she admired and sought to embody.

"I wanna be rich, I wanna be famous, I wanna have lots and lots of money, soar above the clouds. I wanna be free like Nelson Mandela, stand tall like a pyramid, so so courageous. No place I'd rather be, ooh na na na, ooh na na na. There's no place I'd rather be, ooh na na na, ooh na na na."

Tusoli was deeply moved by the lyrics of *Sauti Sol's* hit song. As she sang along with the crowd, the words *"I wanna be free like Nelson Mandela, stand tall like a pyramid, so so courageous"* struck a chord in her. She realized how much she wanted to be a part of the change in Africa, her home.

Sauti Sol continued to perform as Tusoli danced along to the beat, singing every word of *"Live and Die in Afrika."* She felt inspired by the song's message and its call to be remembered, to make a difference, and to be proud of her heritage.

"I wanna feel love, I wanna be remembered, I wanna go down in history, make my mama proud. The darker the berry, the sweeter the juice, na sitoki nyumbani mwacha mila ni mtumwa. No place I'd rather go, no place I'd rather go. I live and die in Afrika, live and die in Afrika, live and die in Afrika, live and die in Afrika."

Tusoli's voice soared, carrying the rich melodies of her African heritage as she sang from the depths of her heart. With each note, she felt a profound sense of belonging and pride in her identity, surrounded by the vibrant energy of the festival. The concert drew to a close, but Tusoli found herself reluctant to leave, having forged new friendships, tasted exotic cuisines, and embraced the unforgettable moments of the day. As the last echoes of the music faded into the night, Tusoli made her way back to her hotel, her spirit still ablaze with excitement. This was only the beginning of her African adventure, and she eagerly anticipated the wonders that awaited her on the journey ahead.

The following day, she would set off for the southern coast of Kenya to explore the Shimoni caves, eager to add another chapter to her unforgettable African odyssey.

CHAPTER 13
THE SHIMONI SLAVE CAVES

Tusoli woke up to the warm morning sun peeking through the curtains of her hotel room, feeling invigorated. She stretched and took a moment to admire the bustling view of Nairobi's busy streets from her balcony before getting ready for the day. She reflected on her time in the city and felt a deep sense of appreciation for the kind and welcoming people she had met thus far.

After an hour of preparation and packing, Tusoli decided to call her mother.

"Hey mom, how are you?" She greeted her warmly.

"I'm fine, darling. How's Nairobi treating you?" Helena responded.

"Like royalty," Tusoli answered with a grin.

"How was the concert yesterday?" Helena inquired.

"It was everything I hoped for. You should listen to 'Live and Die in Africa'; it's amazing," Tusoli replied.

"Is it on YouTube?" Helena asked.

"Absolutely, mom. Check it out," Tusoli encouraged.

"Don't tell me you want to live and die in Africa just yet," Helena joked.

Tusoli chuckled, "Maybe I do, mom. I feel so at home here, surrounded by my people."

"Mama needs you here in Alabama," Helena reminded her.

"Speaking of Alabama, how's the baking business?" Tusoli asked.

"It's been the best thing ever, dear. I love it every day. I even have new clients almost daily," Helena replied.

"I'm glad, Mom. I can't wait to taste those cakes when I'm back," Tusoli said.

"I'll bake one in the shape of Africa for you. I've been inspired by Natalie Sideserf Cakes on Facebook and YouTube," Helena noted.

"I'm sure it'll be amazing," Tusoli replied.

"What's your plan for today?" Helena asked.

"To soak up some vitamin Sea," Tusoli laughed.

"Finally, the Shimoni caves and some vitamin Sea," Helena chuckled.

"I'm thrilled, mom. I've dreamed of this for so long," Tusoli said.

"Have fun and take lots of photos. I want to see what it's like. I loved the Masai Mara pictures and videos," Helena said.

"I'll flood your phone with pictures, Mum. Don't worry. I have to check out now. My flight is at 11 a.m. Bye, mother," Tusoli said.

"Stay safe, girl. Bye. I love you," Helena replied.

Tusoli was whisked away from the heart of the city to Wilson Airport, a short 20-minute drive away. She had chartered a Jumbo jet craft to take her to Diani Airstrip in Ukunda, nestled along the picturesque southern coast of Kenya. As the plane ascended gracefully into the azure sky, Tusoli found herself drawn to the cockpit window, captivated by the breathtaking panorama unfolding below. Nairobi's sprawling cityscape stretched out beneath her, juxtaposed against the verdant expanse of Nairobi National Park. The descent was equally enchanting as Tusoli caught her first glimpse of the sparkling waters of the Indian Ocean and the pristine, ivory-white beaches that lined the Kenyan south coast. She disembarked from the plane and was greeted by her awaiting Akothee Safari Van whisking her to the resort, eager to begin her exploration of the historic slave caves that awaited her.

That evening, Tusoli indulged in the sandy beach and the crystal-clear waters of the Indian Ocean. She delighted in a sumptuous feast of exotic seafood and paired it with a vintage wine as a band played music that stirred memories of her time with Jonathan in Africatown. The memories felt fresh, as if they had happened just yesterday. Though she missed him dearly, she didn't allow herself to dwell on it, as the memory of Karina reminded her to stay present in the moment.

The next morning, Tusoli stepped out of the hotel lobby, radiating style in a crisp white t-shirt, paired with rugged blue pants that hugged her frame perfectly. With a black hat perched jauntily atop her head and golden shades shielding her eyes from the sun, she exuded an air of effortless coolness.

Spotting her safari van waiting patiently for her, Tusoli wasted no time in making her way over, anticipation bubbling within her. With a quick hop inside, she settled into the comfortable interior, her excitement palpable as she embarked on her long-awaited journey to the Shimoni Slave Caves. The thought of Abisai's print still lingering there added to her excitement. She couldn't wait to see the mysterious caves and to learn more about the history and stories hidden within their walls.

Upon reaching the site, Tusoli's eyes caught sight of a piece of wood engraved with the words, *"Welcome to the Shimoni Slave Caves Historical Site Community Project."* She realized that she had finally arrived at her destination. The driver paid her entry fee, and she was introduced to a knowledgeable guide who would lead her into the caves and educate her on its historical significance dating back several centuries.

"Vipi ndugu, Nina huyu mwanadada wa kizungu, mgeni wangu angependa kuelewa historia za Mahali hapa, je unaweza kumfahamisha?" The driver asked the guide in native Swahili language, which roughly translated to "Hello brother, I have a tourist guest who would like to know the history of this place. Could you enlighten her?"

"Naam ndugu, ndiyo kazi yangu hiyo, ni shilingi elfu moja tu," the guide happily replied. which translated to "Yes brother, that is my job. It is only 10 dollars."

Tusoli and the guide descended the steps that led into the Shimoni Caves by the seashore, the driver staying behind, perhaps having brought many guests here before as part of his job. "Enjoy your tour," he called out after them with a smile.

Tusoli trailed closely behind her guide as they descended the steps leading to the cave. Every step she took, she felt the weight of history resting on her shoulders, the agony and torment that had occurred in this exact spot many decades ago. The air felt thick with the energy of the past, and Tusoli couldn't help but be overcome with emotion. She closed her eyes and inhaled deeply, attempting to calm her nerves. She envisioned Abisai, shackled and dragged into the caves, his expression wrought with terror and hopelessness. The sounds of pandemonium and upheaval, like that of the wildebeest migration in the Mara, filled her ears, and she could hear the cries of women and children who were snatched from their homes and forcibly thrust into the dark abyss.

The weight of history and the gravity of the situation weighed heavily on her as she thought of the unimaginable horrors that took place in the very slave caves she was headed into. Her heart ached with empathy and sorrow for the countless lives lost, and the families torn apart. She couldn't help but feel overwhelmed with emotion as she struggled to come to terms with the scale of inhumane treatment that occurred in this very spot. The tears welled up in her eyes as she contemplated the immense pain and suffering that the people had to endure.

"This is the entrance into the caves" the guide interrupted her imagination.

Tusoli's voice trembled with emotion as she posed a question that weighed heavily on her heart, "How many innocent lives had to endure this hell?"

The guide met her gaze with a solemn expression, his words heavy with the weight of history. "Thousands upon thousands, my lady," he replied. "Men, women, children—all crammed into these caves like cattle, awaiting their fate at the hands of merciless traders."

The air felt heavy and suffocating as she stepped into the cave, as if trying to convey the weight of the past. She could feel the darkness closing in on her, like a physical presence. Her footsteps faltered as she imagined the chains and shackles that once bound the enslaved, their cries echoing through the cavernous chambers.

Tusoli stopped for a moment, trying to steady her breath and calm her racing heart. She closed her eyes and imagined Abisai, shackled in this very cave, waiting for his fate to be decided. The image was so vivid, she could almost feel his presence. She took a step forward, her eyes now adjusting to the darkness. She could see the rough walls of the cave, the water dripping from the ceiling. It was all so surreal, and she felt a surge of emotions washing over her - anger, sadness, despair. For Tusoli, this was not just a tourist attraction. It was a reminder of the suffering her ancestors had to endure. She felt a deep connection to this place, and the weight of it all threatened to overwhelm her. With each step, Tusoli felt as though she was bearing witness to the ghosts of the past, their voices echoing in the darkness. She couldn't shake the feeling of foreboding that hung in the air, a silent reminder of the atrocities that had taken place within these walls.

Her heart sank as she noticed the rusty shackles on the walls of the cave. Before she could even ask her guide, he spoke up, as if reading her mind.

"The rusty shackles you see on these walls were used to hold chains that ran through them, binding the ankles and wrists of the poor slaves that were captured," he explained.

"The slaves-on-transit were shackled and then fastened on the metal hooks on the cave walls to hinder their movement, awaiting slave dhows to ship them to Zanzibar, which was the main slave market on the East African Coast."

Tusoli's body shrank, and she felt goosebumps rise on her skin. She couldn't imagine the pain Abisai had gone through in those chains and shackles. Her voice trembled as she spoke, "Wow, that must have been excruciating." She audibly caught her breath.

Tusoli trudged on behind her guide, her footing unsteady, on the uneven and jagged terrain of the cave. As they moved deeper, the air grew danker and the darkness seemed to close in around her. She stumbled, her heart racing with fear and disbelief that hundreds of people were held captive in such conditions. Suddenly, her guide switched on his spotlight, illuminating the way ahead. It was as if he was signaling to her that the worst was yet to come, and her anxiety skyrocketed. The darkness that enveloped her was suffocating.

She felt an eerie and portentous stillness. She could feel some sort of foreshadowing evil.

"Don't be scared" Her custodian assured

"What's at the end of the cave?" Tusoli asked

"Wait, you'll see" the guide replied

He shone his spotlight on a stone and said "You see these stone tanks? This is where they were immersed and fed on dates and nothing else"

"Just dates?" She asked

"Yes, they would feed on dates before the Arab ships arrived"

"So where did ships take them after that?" Tusoli asked again

Guide replied, "They would be shipped to Zanzibar, which was the biggest slave market on the east African shoreline, from there different merchants bought slaves and took them to other countries as they pleased"

Tusoli's voice quivered as she spoke, "It's so dark in here and I can hear water coming. What's that sound?"

"That's the ocean," replied the guide. "This cave system extends further into the sea."

The ominous rumblings from the ocean made Tusoli's heart race with fear.

"We should turn back now. There are many bats past this point, but I believe you have seen enough to understand the gravity of what occurred here," said the guide.

Tusoli nodded in agreement. "Yes, let's turn back. I feel like I have relived the horrors of slavery in its original setting, right here at Shimoni, where my ancestor Abisai came from."

The guide noted Tusoli's interest in learning more about the history of slavery and suggested, "I have met many people like you. If you're eager to delve deeper into the topic, you should visit Zanzibar. It was the largest slave trade market on the East African coast."

"Tusoli responded, "I definitely want to explore Zanzibar. I've heard some mentions of its historical significance in relation to the slave trade."

Emerging from the depths of the cave, Tusoli took a moment to collect herself, her eyes scanning the horizon as she grappled with the enormity of what she had just experienced. The scars of the past ran deep, but she was determined to honor the memory of those who had suffered by bearing witness to their stories.

"Could you tell me the meaning of Shimoni?" Tusoli inquired.

The guide replied, "Shimoni means *the place of the hole* in Swahili. The village got its name from the natural caves that were formed by forces of nature millions of years ago along the seashore."

The name Shimoni—took on a new significance, a reminder of the gaping wound that had been inflicted upon humanity within these very caves.

As the sun dipped below the horizon, casting a warm glow over the landscape, the driver greeted Tusoli and her companion upon their return from their journey into the depths of the Shimoni caves.

"Finally, you're back. It must have been a long trip," the driver remarked, his voice tinged with concern.

"It was indeed a long journey into a dark past," Tusoli replied solemnly, her thoughts still lingering on the haunting echoes of history.

"I'm sure you learned a lot," the driver offered, his tone sympathetic.

"I did," Tusoli confirmed, a somber nod accompanying her words. Turning to the guide, she expressed her gratitude for his patience and insight before bidding him farewell.

With a heavy heart and a newfound appreciation for the resilience of the human spirit, Tusoli prepared to leave for yet another expedition that awaited her.

CHAPTER 14
ZANZIBAR EXPEDITION

Having been deeply moved by her visit to Shimoni, Tusoli's thirst for knowledge of the slave trade in East Africa had only grown stronger. She was determined to uncover the history and stories of those who had been affected by this dark period in time. At sunrise, Tusoli checked out of her hotel and embarked on her journey, eager to learn and to honor those whose lives had been impacted by the brutal slave trade. With her bags packed and her heart heavy, Tusoli set out for Zanzibar, once known to be the largest slave trade market on the East African shoreline.

She settled into her seat aboard the Kenya Airways Aircraft, fastening her seatbelt and gazing out of the window as the plane taxied down the runway. With a sudden burst of energy, the jet engines roared to life, propelling the aircraft into the sky. Tusoli took in the breathtaking views below, filled with anticipation for what lay ahead. For three hours, the flight was smooth, and Tusoli passed the time by reading a book and listening to music.

As they approached Zanzibar, she leaned closer to the window, eagerly taking in the sight of the crystal-clear waters and sandy beaches of the island. The plane landed smoothly, and Tusoli's heart swelled with excitement as she gathered her belongings and made her way off the aircraft. She couldn't wait to explore Zanzibar and learn more about the island's role in the history of slavery. The thought of learning the rich culture and traditions of the region filled her with curiosity.

The following day, Tusoli sought out information about the island's involvement in the slave trade and enlisted the help of a guide. Together, they journeyed to the Mangapwani Coral Caverns, a site located north of Zanzibar's Stone Town, where remnants of this dark period still lingered. She was astounded upon reaching the entrance of the cavern. It was a vast, natural underground cave inside a coral reef that was much larger than the Shimoni caves. In contrast to the Shimoni caves, Tusoli noticed that this cave had a natural spring with fresh water, which made it an ideal hiding spot for slaves after slavery was abolished in Zanzibar in 1873.

Tusoli and her guide ventured deeper into the cave; the atmosphere became dank and darker, prompting the guide to use his torch to illuminate their path.

He explained, "This cave was used to hide slaves who were destined for a journey of no return. After the slave trade was officially abolished, it was owned by a wealthy Arab man named *Hamed Salim El Hathy,* who had acquired many slaves to work on his plantations."

Tusoli asked, "How long did the slaves stay here?"

The guide replied, "They stayed here for up to three weeks until the ships arrived to transport them."

Tusoli was shocked to learn that the cave was an astounding 100-meter-long stone staircase that led to a dark bottom where a colony of bats now resided. To the left of the cave, the guide showed her a secret passage from which the slaves were led out to the sea and onto waiting dhows. At the lowest point of the cave, there was a pool of fresh water.

The guide then directed Tusoli to turn back so that he could show her the *Zanzibar slave chambers.*

After reaching the top and exiting the cave, Tusoli felt utterly exhausted. Unlike Shimoni, where the descent was not steep, *Mangapwani Coral Cavern* was a long flight of stairs and the climb back up had taken a toll on her. She was panting heavily and felt like she might have a cardiac arrest. She took a few deep breaths and drank some water, trying to recover from the exertion. The guide waited patiently for her, understanding how taxing the climb could be. Tusoli couldn't believe that people had to endure this kind of hardship and cruelty as they were being transported to slavery.

She took a few breaths before they got swallowed into the dense cover of indigenous trees into the next slave cavern. The chamber was about three meters wide by fourteen meters long and three and a half meters deep. The guide proceeded, "The slaves came here by boat from Bagamoyo, and up to a hundred of them were packed together in this cavern, enduring the sweltering coastal heat for days as they waited for merchant ships to take them to Omani slave markets and beyond."

Entering the Zanzibar slave chambers, Tusoli was confronted with the harsh reality of confinement. The stifling heat and cramped conditions painted a grim picture of the hardships endured by slaves awaiting shipment.

Tusoli asked, "How did they manage to survive in these conditions? It's already so hot here. How could so many people not suffocate in here?"

The guide replied, "Actually, some did die due to the conditions here."

How could humanity have allowed such atrocities to occur? The answer lay buried within the walls of these slave caves. It sickened her to think that people were once okay with trading humans like commodities. It was all told by the *whispers of the lave caves.*

Whispers of the Slave Caves
Deep within the cave's dark depths
A haunting silence reigns
Echoes of the past still linger
Whispers of unspeakable pain.
The walls are etched with stories
Of those who suffered here
A tragic chapter in history
That fills our hearts with fear.
Chained and shackled, they were led
To the ships that lay in wait
Taken far from their homeland
To an unknown and cruel fate.
Their voices still echo in the cave
Their tears still fall like rain
Their spirits haunt this solemn place
Their memories cause us pain.
We walk among the ruins
With heavy hearts and solemn mind
Remembering the lives that were lost
to the greed of humankind.
We vow to never forget

The atrocities that were done
And to honor the memories of those
Whose fight for freedom had just begun.
We stand in silence, in reverence
For the brave souls who suffered here
May their legacy live on forever
And their spirits find peace, without fear.

Tusoli's exploration of Zanzibar was a journey through time. Visiting the well-preserved former slave markets, she bore witness to the harrowing legacy of the slave trade. Yet, amidst the echoes of suffering, she found solace in the resilience of those who fought against such injustices.

After bearing witness to the harrowing past, Tusoli sought solace in the vibrant present. She embarked on a spice tour in Kizimbani, reveling in the rich aromas and flavors of Zanzibar's renowned spices. A horse ride in Kama offered a moment of tranquility, as she let the gentle rhythm of the horse's hooves carry her through the picturesque landscape.

Visiting the Sultan Persian Bath in Kidichi, Tusoli immersed herself in the island's cultural heritage, marveling at the intricate architecture and storied history of the ancient bathhouse. A walk through the Masingini Natural Forest Reserve in Bububu provided a refreshing escape into nature, a stark contrast to the weight of the past she had carried with her.

Through each experience, Tusoli discovered the resilience of the human spirit and the enduring beauty of Zanzibar's landscapes and traditions. As she bid farewell to the island, she carried with her a newfound appreciation for the power of history to shape the present and inspire change.

"The trip to Africa is totally worth it, everything is pure magic." She said to herself.

As the African sun dipped below the horizon, painting the sky in hues of orange and gold, Tusoli made her way back to her hotel in Zanzibar's Stone Town. Eager to unwind and relax, she headed to the white sandy beach to enjoy the picturesque views of the blue sea, just as she loved it. Settling into a cozy spot on the shore, Tusoli savored the flavors of the ocean, indulging in the freshest seafood Zanzibar had to offer. As she dined al fresco, the gentle rhythm of the waves provided the perfect soundtrack to her evening, a soothing melody that calmed her soul and ignited her senses.

In an instant, her life played out before her like a vivid film. She saw herself as a child, carefree and full of wonder; her teenage years, filled with laughter and wisdom shared with her father; moments with her best friend Karina; and tender times with Jonathan. She had known the highs of abundance and luck, and the lows of pain and heartbreak. Her experiences spanned the spectrum of life's extremes, and she felt a deep gratitude for where she stood now.

As she sat there, tears glistening in her eyes, she looked up at the sky, whispering a heartfelt prayer, affirming her strength and resilience.

" I stand as a sovereign before this vast and mighty sea, this profound creation.

As this sea offers its boundless bounty, so shall my life be filled with abundance.

As this sea never knows lack, so shall I never face deprivation.

As this sea brims with fullness, so shall my life be complete and fulfilled.

As this sea's waves rise and surge with power, so shall the forces of the universe rise to defend me against all who wish harm upon me, my family, and my descendants.

As this sea embodies the essence of plentitude, so shall my life be enriched with love, prosperity, and success.

Amen."

SHE WATCHED AS THE sun turned into a golden half sphere, sinking below the horizon, casting a warm glow over the blue sea. The sound of the waves and the refreshing sea breeze created a tranquil atmosphere, allowing her to fully relax and enjoy the moment.

The Blue Sea

Oh, the splendor of her majesty,
The blue sea, she who reigns supreme,
Her beauty an eternal melody,
A symphony that plays a lifelong theme.
Beneath her boundaries lies a world of wonder,
A sight to behold, an ethereal treasure trove,
A surreal journey that drags you under,
A place where you discover a love that you never knew.
She harbors tales of human grandeur,
Of explorers and adventurers who braved her depths,
And yet there's so much more, so much grander,
A richness that even the poor can attest.
In her calm, she offers a veil of serenity,
A haven for the weary to find their peace,
But in her storms, she screams with such ferocity,
That even the halls of heaven may cower and cease.
Her waters are not to be taken lightly,
For her wrath can sweep you off your feet,
Her moods, at times, can be quite frightening,
A force to be reckoned with, an entity that's hard to defeat.
Oh, the Blue Sea, you are a masterpiece,
A creation so divine, a work of art so grand,
You stir the depths of my soul with such ease,
And with you, I find a love that's truly grand.
Am in Love with you Blue Sea

As Tusoli turned, she caught sight of a lovestruck Romeo whom she had gently rebuffed just a week ago. She couldn't help but feel a flutter in her heart as she met his gaze, and wondered how he saw her in comparison to the Blue Sea.

"Have you been following me?" Tusoli questioned, feeling a bit uneasy.

Leonardo shook his head. "No, not at all. I never imagined I'd bump into you again here in Zanzibar. Who could have foreseen this chance encounter?" he replied with a hopeful smile.

Tusoli replied, "What are you doing here, in Zanzibar Leonardo"

Leonardo's heart was racing as he spoke to Tusoli, his eyes never leaving her face. He couldn't believe his luck to have met her again on the beautiful shores of Zanzibar. The more they spoke, the more he felt a powerful connection to her, as though they had been acquainted for ages.

"I came here on holiday," he explained. "My tour guide recommended this place to me when I was in Masai Mara."

Tusoli nodded, her eyes sparkling with interest. "And you've been here for three days?"

Leonardo nodded. "Yes, I was planning to leave tomorrow morning, but I decided to come to the beach and catch some final waves. And here you are, again."

Tusoli smiled, her heart racing just as fast as Leonardo's.

"What a coincidence. We didn't meet again at Masai Mara."

Leonardo shook his head regretfully, "No, I arrived too late at the camp. I was hoping to find you there."

Tusoli's eyebrows rose in surprise, "Looking for me? Why?"

Leonardo hesitated for a moment, then decided to take a chance, "When I saw you boarding that plane in Georgia, I knew I had to talk to you. I must say, I switched seats with the lady who was supposed to actually sit next to you, it cost me 100 dollars but I couldn't find the courage to say hello to you until the aircraft landed. And then I lost you in the crowd."

Tusoli's eyes widened in surprise. "I had no idea," she said softly. "I was going through a tough time then, so I didn't notice much."

Leonardo's heart went out to her, "A tough time you say? Do you mind sharing?" he asked gently. "We could sit by the bar overlooking the ocean and have some wine."

Tusoli's face lit up, "I miss some wine, actually. Not a bad idea at all."

They strolled to the hotel's front, a stunning view of the ocean with palm trees surrounding them. At the open and secluded bar, Leonardo pulled out a stool for her. They settled down and gazed at the vast blue sea, the setting sun sinking into the horizon, beckoning the stars to come out. The waters reflected the star's light, creating infinite waves that played a symphony on the sandy beach, taking her down memory lane.

"This setting reminds me of someone" she said.

Leonardo quipped, "Your boyfriend, I must say."

Tusoli revealed, "My ex-boyfriend, a sweet-talking guy, just like you, who got my best friend pregnant and proposed to me simultaneously. He even planned a wedding, unaware that the abortion he plotted with her was unsuccessful."

Leonardo was stunned, "What? That's outrageous. You're beautiful, and any man would be lucky to have you. Maybe it was just a mistake"

Tusoli remarked, "You can't be certain about that. Why would he continue to meet with her repeatedly?

"So, it wasn't just a one-time thing?" Leonardo was taken aback.

"No," Tusoli replied, "She even visited him multiple times while I was working in Auburn."

Leonardo was shocked, "How could your best friend do that to you?"

Tusoli responded, "I don't blame her, really. Karina was a good person, but he used her. He wanted to dump her, but she ended up getting pregnant."

"It sounds like something out of a fiction novel. Are you still with him? What happened to your best friend?" Leonardo couldn't believe it.

Tusol added, "Apparently, he must be serving a long jail term by now, and there's no way we could ever be together after that incident. My heart was crushed into a million pieces Leo."

Leonardo, surprised, asked, "I'm sorry to ask, but he went to jail for breaking your heart?"

Tusoli laughed bitterly. "Really Leo? No, not that. Actually, he killed my best friend after a heated argument. She hit her head on the sink tub after he pushed her. It was a sinister accident."

Leonardo's expression changed to one of sadness and sympathy, "I'm so sorry for what you went through. That's truly terrible."

[Their conversation was interrupted by a waitress who approached their table.]

"Can I get you anything?" she asked.

"Yes, Tusoli would like a bottle of red or white wine?" Leonardo said, pointing at her.

"I actually prefer red, but a change is good, right?" Tusoli interjected.

"Okay, we'll have a bottle of vintage white wine and two bottles of cold Tusker Malt and a bottle of water, please," Leonardo said to the waitress.

Tusoli furrowed her brow, "Tusker Malt? Is that some type of beer?"

"Yes, it's one of the smoothest beers I've ever had here. Very well brewed," Leonardo explained.

The waitress returned with a bottle of white wine and a wine glass, along with two bottles of Tusker Malt. After serving them, Leonardo poured the wine into Tusoli's glass and they raised their glasses for a toast.

"Welcome, cheers," he said.

"To what?" Tusoli asked with a smile, raising her glass.

"To meeting a stranger again and making new friends," he replied cheerfully.

They clinked glasses and took a sip.

"Why white wine today?" Leonardo asked.

"I think it's time for a new chapter in my life, new memories, and new experiences. And when I go back to Auburn, I want to associate it with white wine," Tusoli answered.

"Red wine brings back memories that I would otherwise like to bury and forget." She added.

Tusoli noticed Leonardo's gaze and felt a tinge of shyness, but she also couldn't deny the attraction she felt towards him too. She took another sip of wine to gather her thoughts and then spoke.

"You know, I never thought I'd be sitting here, in this beautiful place, with a stranger who has become a friend so fast," she said, breaking the silence.

Leonardo smiled, feeling his heart race at her words. "Life is full of surprises, isn't it?" he replied.

Tusoli nodded, taking another sip of wine. "It certainly is," she said softly.

"I came to Zanzibar to break away from the monotonous and dull life in Georgia and to see what life brings me. And here I am, sitting next to the most beautiful woman on the planet." Leonardo flattered her.

Tusoli blushed and replied, "Georgia must have been boring for you. It's interesting to meet someone like you not only once, but again here we are, in Zanzibar, overlooking the beautiful blue sea and a sandy beach. Although, I could be a gold digger or maybe a serial killer for all you know.

"Wait, serial killer no, gold digger? Maybe, but serial killer?" Leonardo said as they both laughed it out.

Tusoli added, "Gold digger? We'll see about that. Well, I'm not a serial killer, don't freak out."

Leonardo replied, "If you were, I would surely be ready to visit my maker. You are irresistible, to say the least."

Tusoli felt flattered by Leonardo. He always had a way of making her laugh, "You have a way with words, Leonardo. Your compliments are as smooth as the Tusker Malt you are drinking, my guess."

Leonardo was flattered, "I can't help it, Tusoli. You have a light in your eyes that brightens up this whole place."

"You're making me blush again. But I have to admit, this place has a darkness to it that I can't ignore." She added

Leonardo responded, "What do you mean?"

"The slave caves. The history of this place is a constant reminder of the evil that humans are capable of." Tusoli clarified.

Leonardo responded, "I know. It's heartbreaking to think about the suffering that happened here."

Tusoli added, "It's more than just heartbreaking, Leonardo. It's a reminder of how far we've come and how far we still have to go. We can never forget the atrocities that happened in the slave trade era."

Leonardo nodded in agreement, his gaze softening with understanding. "You're right," he replied. "It's our responsibility to remember and honor the lives that were lost here and anywhere else, and strive for equality in today's society."

Tusoli's eyes met his, "Exactly," she said. "That's why I came here, to honor their lives, and to remind myself of the work that still needs to be done to end modern day slavery and inequality."

Leonardo's admiration for Tusoli only grew as he listened to her heartfelt words. "I admire your dedication, Tusoli," he said sincerely.

"Thank you, Leonardo," Tusoli replied with a grateful smile.

As the conversation shifted to lighter topics, Leonardo shared his plan for the next day. "Tomorrow I'll be visiting *Avicennia Island*," he announced. "Join me."

Curious, Tusoli leaned in, her interest piqued. "What's on the island? Is it nearby?"

"It's a hidden gem," Leonardo explained, his eyes lighting up with excitement. "A stunningly beautiful secluded island in Mombasa, Kenya, that's perfect for kayaking."

Tempted by the idea, Tusoli's curiosity got the best of her. "Sounds amazing," she said. "Count me in."

"Great," Leonardo replied with a grin. "I'll pick you up tomorrow morning at the hotel's entrance, then we can head to the airport together."

"Sure thing," Tusoli said, her smile widening. "I'll take my wine to my room then. Thanks for the company and the invitation." With a warm farewell, she added, "Have a good night, Leonardo."

Leonardo returned her smile, "Goodnight, Tusoli," he said softly. "Thank you for having me."

He walked away briskly to his hotel about fifteen meters from there with hopes that Tusoli won't slip again from him this time.

Probably to cover her indecision on whether to join Leonardo the following day or just keep on with her own itinerary, Tusoli stayed a while longer at the bar and drank her wine gently as the sea breeze and the waves coalesced to treat her to a serenading in situ experience as the night sky glimmered with its infinite stars.

CHAPTER 15
LOVE STRUCK ROMEO

Leonardo's plea for love echoed in the serene island of *Avicennia*, amidst the gentle lapping of the waves. Tusoli, still reeling from the pain of heartbreak, listened intently to his words, her heart heavy with apprehension.

"If you allow me, I promise to love you with a gentleness and tenderness you've never experienced," Leonardo implored, his voice filled with sincerity and longing.

Tusoli understood the allure of his offer, yet she remained cautious, mindful of the scars that still lingered within her. She knew the risks that came with opening her heart again, but there was something about Leonardo's earnestness that stirred a flicker of hope within her battered soul. Tusoli's voice quivered with vulnerability as she opened up to Leonardo, "Love is a big commitment for me at the moment Leonardo, I lost my best friend because of love, I was intertwined in its web and am still trying to process and accept that everything is changed now"

Leonardo listened attentively, "I know it's not been easy for you, but I come here with pure intentions, let me help you get through it." He said to her.

Tusoli hesitated, her thoughts swirling with apprehension. "I don't know if I'm ready, Leonardo. Let's take each moment as it comes, one step at a time. For now, I find solace in the fact that we are no longer strangers. Perhaps, if our paths cross again, things might be different."

Leonardo nodded understandingly. "I respect your hesitations, Tusoli. I'll be here, waiting for you, whenever you're ready to take that step forward. Until then, maybe we can cherish the connection we've forged and see where it leads us."

"I don't want to lead you on, Leonardo," she began, her tone tinged with caution. "My past is complicated, and I'm not sure if I'm ready for anything serious at the moment."

Leonardo met her honesty with understanding, his response gentle yet reassuring. "I understand, Tusoli. Let's simply embrace this moment—the beauty of this sunset, the warmth of our conversation. Let's be present and savor the magic of this moment together."

Tusoli nodded, a small smile playing on her lips. "Let's enjoy the sun set, then probably head back to the hotel so I can rest and book my flight tomorrow. I still feel weary from the Zanzibar jetlag and Zambia is waiting for me."

Tusoli noticed the intensity of Leonardo's gaze and averted her eyes, feeling a bit uneasy. She took another sip of her coffee, trying to calm her nerves. She could feel the chemistry between them, but she wasn't sure if it was just a fleeting attraction or something more.

Leonardo found himself drawn to Tusoli's vulnerability, and he couldn't resist the urge to touch her hand. She looked up at him, surprised, but didn't pull away. They sat like that for a few moments, just holding hands, lost in their own thoughts. They headed to the Van but Tusoli felt a pang of sadness in her heart, knowing that she might never see him again, but perhaps their paths would cross again someday just like they always did.

Meanwhile, Leonardo was consumed by his emotions, overwhelmed by the depth of his connection with Tusoli. He longed to express his feelings for her, to make her understand the depth of his affection, but words seemed inadequate to convey the intensity of what he truly felt. Despite his earnest efforts, Leonardo couldn't shake off the feeling that the timing wasn't quite right. Perhaps, he mused, their paths would cross again in Alabama, and by then, Tusoli would be ready to open her heart to him. Or maybe she still needed time to heal from her heartbreak and mourn for her friend.

The *Avicennia Island* was breathtaking. Tusoli marveled at the grandeur of her ancestral motherland, wondering if her fellow African descendants in the United States could ever experience such magnificence. The Island, located off the coast of Mombasa, Kenya, is a hidden gem renowned for its stunning natural beauty and rich cultural heritage. Named after the Avicennia marina, a species of mangrove tree found abundantly in the area, the island offers visitors a unique and unforgettable experience.

One of the island's main attractions is its pristine beaches, which boast powdery white sands and crystal-clear turquoise waters. Visitors can indulge in a variety of water activities such as swimming, snorkeling, and kayaking, allowing them to explore the vibrant marine life that thrives in the surrounding coral reefs. Avicennia Island is also home to lush mangrove forests, which serve as important ecosystems for a wide range of plant and animal species. Guided tours through the mangroves offer visitors the opportunity to learn about the island's biodiversity and conservation efforts.

In addition to its natural wonders, Avicennia Island is steeped in history and culture. The island's inhabitants, primarily of Swahili descent, have preserved traditional customs and practices that date back centuries. Visitors can immerse themselves in the local culture by participating in traditional dance performances, sampling authentic Swahili cuisine, and visiting historical sites such as ancient ruins and mosques.

Avicennia Island offers a tranquil retreat from the hustle and bustle of city life, where visitors can reconnect with nature, explore rich cultural heritage, and create lasting memories amidst stunning surroundings.

Just a dream

"Hey Tusoli, why did you do this to me" She heard a voice addressing her, loud and clear.

"What are you doing here Karina, aren't you supposed to be dead?" Tusoli responded in shock.

"You made Jonathan do this to me, if it wasn't for you, I'd still be alive. Jonathan never loved you, he loved me. Only me Tusoli"

Tusoli jolted up in bed, gasping for air,
Her mind was trapped
in that haunting nightmare.
Karina's accusing voice echoed in her head,
Filling her with fear and dread.
She tried to shake off the feeling of guilt,
Knowing that it was all just a dream she built.

But the weight of her conscience still remained,
As she wondered if she's the one to blame.
Tusoli tried to calm her racing heart,
And soothe her mind before she fell apart.
She reminded herself it was just a dream,
And Karina's accusations were not what they seem.

Tusoli's eyes were wide open, her breath ragged from the vivid and disturbing dream that had just ripped her from a deep sleep. Her heart pounded with fear and anxiety as she tried to shake off the effects of the dream. She had heard Karina's voice accusing her of being responsible for her death and blaming her for Jonathan's infidelity.

Tusoli shuddered at the thought and tried to calm herself down, reminding herself that it was just a dream. She immediately called her mother to tell her about it.

"I used to have bad dreams too, dear. Sometimes they come from something that's been bothering you for a long time," Helena told her.

"What should I do, Mom? I can't even sleep again, it felt so real," Tusoli replied.

Helena said, "Perhaps you've been feeling guilty about Karina's death, and that's why you had that nightmare. Why don't you go to the hotel bar and get a glass of wine? It might help you sleep better."

Tusoli said, "Okay, Mom, I think I need that. What time is it in Auburn now?"

Helena replied, "It's 11am, dear. I'm already at the bakery."

Tusoli said, "Okay, mum, let me stretch to the lounge area then probably try to get some sleep."

After a restful night's sleep, Tusoli woke up feeling refreshed and energized. She took a hot shower and then decided to wear a *dera* dress she bought in Diani, which is a traditional attire for the Swahili coastal women. When she wore the dress, she blended in perfectly with the local culture and traditions.

She headed downstairs, where a sumptuous breakfast was served to her before Leonardo joined in shortly after.

"Morning Tusoli," he greeted her.

"Good morning, Leonardo," she replied.

Leonardo pulled up a chair and sat at the same table as Tusoli.

The air between them was quiet for a moment until the waiter interrupted.

"What can I serve you, sir?" the waiter asked.

"Two eggs, bacon, and buttered bread, please," he replied.

"How was your night, Tusoli." Leonardo broke the silence.

"It was full of nightmares. I couldn't sleep well. I had to come down to the lounge. That's when I saw you coming in at the doorway with your mistress, you guys were so drunk" she responded.

"You let her out so early? Wasn't she having breakfast?" Tusoli added.

"Actually, no. But it's not what it looked like. I feel so embarrassed," Leonardo explained.

"You don't have to be embarrassed, and you don't need to explain anything to me, Leonardo. We're not dating," Tusoli said while smiling.

"Well, what were your nightmares about?" Leonardo asked moving away from the topic.

"Karina. She came to me in a dream and blamed me for her death," Tusoli replied.

"You don't believe it was your fault, right?" Leonardo questioned.

"Maybe if I didn't get involved with Jonathan, she would still be alive. He tortured her because of me"

"Well, you can't blame yourself for things you can't change. It was unfortunate she died so young." Leonardo tried to comfort her.

"I don't even want to think about it, Leonardo. It breaks my heart every time" Tusoli admitted.

"Forget about it. Maybe we can go somewhere, and you can relax your mind, it's your last day in Kenya" Leonardo suggested.

Tusoli suggested an idea, "I was researching the Northern Kenya coast and found out about *Robinson island*. It's about 40 minutes from Malindi and three hours from here. We can go explore and be back in time."

Leonardo agreed, "That sounds great! I'll call the driver and inform him of our plans. Meet me back here in thirty minutes?."

Tusoli responded, "Okay, I'll be here before you."

They both returned to their respective rooms to get ready for their trip to *Robinson island* on the Northern coast.

After a lengthy drive, they arrived at the entrance of *Robinson Island,* where they stopped to admire the hippos and flocks of pink flamingos at the mouth of the Sabaki River. They then proceeded to *Che Shale,* the famous *Golden Beach,* where the sand was speckled with pyrite, giving it a golden hue. Tusoli was awestruck when she touched the sand and her hands sparkled with gold dust.

They continued their journey and passed by the largest salt pans in Kenya, where natural pools sparkled in an array of colors, from pristine white to delicate shades of pink creating a mesmerizing natural spectacle. Leaving their van behind, they climbed into a pirogue, a traditional wooden canoe, ready to embark on the next leg of their journey.

The friendly local man named Caronte skillfully navigated the native canoe through the calm waters, standing at the stern of the boat and singing beautiful Swahili lyrics. His voice was filled with emotion as he sang the timeless words of "Malaika," a song by Miriam Makeba.

"Malaika, nakupenda Malaika

(Angel, I love you, my angel)

Malaika, nakupenda Malaika

(Angel, I love you, my angel)

Ningekua na mali wee, ningekuoa dada

(If only i had wealth, I would marry you, sister)"

His voice, like a gentle breeze, carried the heartfelt words across the lagoon, blending seamlessly with the natural melody of the sea and the gentle splash of the paddle, creating a unique and mesmerizing music that filled the air.

"Nashindwa na mali sina wee

(I am overcome without riches)

Ningekuoa Malaika

(I would marry you, my angel)

Nashindwa na mali sina wee

(I am overcome without riches)

Ningekuoa Malaika

(I would marry you, my angel)"

Tusoli on learning the song, moved by the raw emotion in Caronte's voice, couldn't resist joining in, her own voice adding depth and harmony to the enchanting melody:

"Pesa zasumbua roho yangu

(Money troubles my soul)
Pesa zasumbua roho yangu
(Money troubles my soul)
Nami nifanyeje, kijana mwenzio
(What am I to do, my dear fellow)"

Together, their voices created a magical symphony that echoed through the lagoon, captivating Leonardo, evoking a longing for Tusoli in his soul.

After several hours, they finally arrived at *Robinson Island*. Tusoli was completely captivated by the stunning scenery that greeted her.

Here, they were welcomed by a charming Swahili restaurant, nestled amidst lush greenery and made entirely with traditional makuti and mangrove roots. The beach white sand served as its floor, inviting guests to kick off their shoes and truly immerse themselves in the island's natural beauty. The restaurant's open-air design allowed for the gentle sea breeze to cool off the diners as they indulged in the delicious seafood spread, creating a totally unforgettable dining experience. While they sat down to enjoy the delicious meal, the scent of the fresh seafood tantalized their taste buds, and Tusoli couldn't help but take a deep breath in to savor the aroma.

The Robinson crabs were the star of the show, cooked to perfection with a blend of spices that left a lingering taste in their mouths. The prawns were plump and juicy, and the grilled fish flaked off effortlessly with each bite. The lobsters were succulent and buttery, while the oysters were briny and refreshing. The coconut rice was fluffy and fragrant, the sauce added a zing of flavor, and the salads and fruits provided a refreshing balance to the richness of the seafood. The table was a feast for the eyes as well, with vibrant frangipani flowers and bougainvillea decorating the table, making it look like a tropical paradise. As they ate, the sound of the waves lapping against the shore provided a soothing background melody. Tusoli and Leonardo savored each bite, relishing the flavors amidst the beautiful surroundings. It was a truly grateful and memorable moment on Robinson Island.

They basked in the serene atmosphere with the ocean stretching out before them, the sky a vibrant blue, and countless red crabs scurrying along the pristine white beach. Excited to explore more of the island, they embarked on a journey to a place called *Marafa*, also known as *"Hell's Kitchen"* or "Kitchen of the Devil".

Once they arrived, they were in awe of the incredible scenery before them. This natural wonder was unparalleled in all of Africa: a massive canyon, carved out during the Pliocene era, surrounded by towering vertical walls adorned with reddish spires and imposing stone pillars reaching up to a height of 30 meters. Tusoli and Leonardo were both captivated by the beauty of the canyon, and they took their time exploring every nook and cranny.

Marafa, known as Hell's Kitchen, is a natural wonder that truly defies belief. At sunset, the rocks and spires surrounding the large canyon appear to change colors, taking on shades of white, pink, ochre, and red, creating an otherworldly atmosphere. Tusoli was left in awe, feeling like she had been transported to another planet altogether. As they walked through the valleys of the canyon for about an hour, they couldn't help but feel humbled by the sheer magnitude and beauty of this natural wonder.

After their excursion, they returned to the Swahili restaurant where they rested under the twinkling stars, still mesmerized by the day's experiences.

Leonardo remarked, "This is the most stunning thing I have ever seen," and Tusoli replied, "It's breathtaking. I wonder how many more wonders like this are out there waiting to be discovered."

"I wish we had more time," Leonardo lamented.

"Unfortunately, we don't. But I will definitely come back to this country," she said.

They returned to Mombasa, chatting and laughing about the day's adventures. Later that evening, Leonardo and Tusoli met at the hotel lounge.

"At least I can enjoy my last glass of wine in Kenya," Tusoli remarked, swirling her drink.

Leonardo raised his beer. "Well, here's to more adventures and a life full of surprises."

"Cheers to that," Tusoli agreed, clinking her glass against his.

Then, with a playful grin, she teased, "So, Leo, any plans for tonight? Another mysterious rendezvous?"

Leonardo chuckled, but there was a hint of guilt in his eyes. "Come on, Tusoli, you know me better than that. I'm a one-woman kind of guy."

Tusoli's smile faltered slightly. "Oh really? Then what happened last night?"

Leonardo's expression grew sheepish. "Honestly, I don't even remember her name."

Tusoli's playful demeanor faded. "Sounds like a wild night. Was she at least worth the hangover?"

Leonardo shrugged, feeling uncomfortable under Tusoli's gaze. "She was alright, I guess. But nothing compared to the company I have now."

Tusoli forced a smile, but her eyes betrayed a hint of hurt. "Smooth recovery, Leo. But next time, just bring back some pizza instead."

Leonardo chuckled nervously. "Noted. So, are we good?"

Tusoli nodded, but her tone was distant. "Of course, Leo. Am just curious"

"Cheers," he said, raising his glass. "To honesty and good company."

"To honesty and good company," Tusoli echoed, clinking her glass against his, but her laughter sounded forced. As Leonardo watched her, unsure of his chances, he couldn't shake the feeling that he had jeopardized something important between them.

CHAPTER 16
NDOLA SLAVE TREE
ZAMBIA

On a tranquil afternoon in the enchanting city of Lusaka, the rain gently falls from the sky like a symphony of rhythmical beats. Amidst the serene setting, a Kenya Airways Dreamliner gracefully touches down at the magnificent Kenneth Kaunda International Airport, bringing with it a world of adventurers and wanderers.

Tusoli disembarks from the aircraft and hires a tour service van that takes her through the vibrant streets of the city to the luxurious Radisson Blu Grand Hotel. The stunning architecture of the hotel took her breath away, and the warm hospitality of the staff made her feel right at home. She relaxed in the cozy confines of her room and called her mother to share her joy of arriving safely in this wondrous land in yet another quest to follow the prints of her forefather Abisai, and they indulged in a delightful conversation filled with love and laughter. Tusoli spent the next day acquainting herself with the new city and finding out what it hid from the ancient slave trade.

Tusoli set out to explore the enchanting city, filled with a mix of excitement and trepidation. The bustling streets of Lusaka pulsed with life, Every face she passed on the streets, every smile exchanged, held the potential to be a connection to her past. Abisai had married a woman from here and had two children before he was lost to the chains of slavery. As she walked, she couldn't shake the feeling of anticipation tinged with a hint of anxiety. What if she stumbled upon someone who shared her bloodline, someone who could offer a glimpse into her family's past? What if Abisai's descendants were among the vendors selling their wares, or the children playing in the streets? The possibilities were endless, and yet, they also filled her with a sense of unease. But it was when she heard about the mysterious *Ndola slave tree,* located hundreds of kilometers away from Lusaka, that Tusoli knew she simply had to see it for herself.

The thought of visiting such a fascinating and historical site filled her with excitement, and she added it to her growing list of must visit destinations without hesitation. As the sun rose on the following morning, Tusoli boarded a local flight to *Ndola,* her curiosity piqued by the prospect of discovering more about the region's storied past. Her guide led her to the Slave Tree, an enigmatic landmark that stood alone, bereft of the cave systems found elsewhere.

Tusoli's inquisitive mind was immediately captivated by the unusual sight, and she couldn't help but ponder why this tree had been chosen as a symbol of slavery. Learning deeper into the tree's history from her guide, the truth began to unfurl before her. The towering monolith had borne witness to countless atrocities, serving as a symbol of unimaginable suffering for those who had been sold into servitude. The stories of those who had endured this dark chapter of humanity were etched into the very bark of the tree.

Strolling near the center of Ndola along Makoli Avenue, you could be tempted to rest underneath the shady old pod mahogany tree. Its full branches and large leaves created the perfect environment for restful slumber. As huge as it was, with the thick trunk by the edge, it was surrounded by a small fence with an open gate. The residents adorn its large, high branches, always Swaying calmly in the swift Ndola breeze. As calm as it seemed, this was once a haven for Swahili slave traders where they met under its shade to discuss their gruesome transactions.

According to the guide's account, Swahili traders such as *Chipembere, Mwalabu,* and *Chiwala* held councils of war under this tree and sold enslaved people to the *Mambundu* from Angola and beyond. These traders would enslave people themselves or buy people who had been captured by warring local tribes and sell them off into the then thriving slave trade. Many years later, this ancient tree was now a monument to those killed by the barbaric slave trade. For many decades, its branches stood tall against the ravages of time, and its leaves were broad and embracing yet its sagging and hunching appeared to mourn the loss of those whose predicament was plotted right under its shade.

Tusoli stood beneath the ancient Ndola slave tree, her heart heavy with disbelief and sorrow as she learned about the brutal history of the slave trade that had unfolded right where she stood. The thought of people betraying and selling their own into slavery was incomprehensible to her. For a moment, she struggled to hold back her emotions, feeling overwhelmed by the weight of history. She listened to the hush of the tree leaves as they danced with the breeze, carrying with them the echoes of centuries past. As a tear rolled down her left cheek, so too did a flaky leaf from the massive tree fall to the ground. It felt like a poignant sign, as if the enslaved souls of the past were traveling with the wind to grieve alongside her.

After her visit to the Ndola slave tree, Tusoli returned to Lusaka for one more day before embarking on a journey to the awe-inspiring Victoria Falls, a natural wonder that spans across Zimbabwe and Zambia. The falls were a mesmerizing destination that attracted travelers from all over the globe. Tusoli was fortunate to visit during a season of high water levels, allowing her to witness the full glory of the falls. Known as Mosi-oa-Tunya in the Kololo tribe language, which translated to "the smoke that thunders," the falls were a sight to behold.

Approaching the falls, Tusoli felt the thunderous roar and the mist that engulfed the air. Tourists donned their ponchos as they were embraced by the powerful force of the falls. Tusoli indulged in the thrill of bungee jumping and helicopter rides above the cascading falls, before concluding her adventure with a fine dining experience along the Zambezi River.

From her table, she was captivated by the panoramic view of the mighty river stretching out for miles, before plummeting 100 meters to create a thunderous cascade of water. The sheer force of the falls filled the air with mist, forming a breathtaking rainbow as the evening sun's rays danced upon the turbulent waters. In that moment, Tusoli felt a surge of emotions as she savored this magical spectacle, one that she would cherish for a lifetime.

CHAPTER 17
FINAL EXPEDITION

Tusoli's departure from Zambia was imminent, her flight to *Benin* scheduled for 2 PM. Though her stay in Zambia had been brief, she felt honored to have visited the country where her possible bloodline could be thriving.. As her luggage was loaded onto the hotel van, she couldn't help but feel a twinge of sadness at leaving so soon. But her excitement for the final leg of her African adventure was palpable, and she eagerly climbed into the van, ready for the journey ahead. The thought of unraveling more layers of her family's history in Benin stirred her soul.

In a matter of minutes, they pulled up at the airport, and Tusoli bid farewell to her Zambian guides. Boarding the plane, she couldn't contain her excitement for what lay ahead in Benin – the very place where her ancestor, Abisai, had been captured and forced onto The Clotilda. After a six-hour flight, she touched down at Cotonou Cadjehoun Airport in Benin, west Africa ready to dive into the next chapter of her journey. She quickly checked into a hotel in the bustling city, eager to shake off the jetlag and embark on her exploration.

The next day, Tusoli woke up to the warm embrace of the tropical sunshine in Cotonou, her spirit buoyant with anticipation for the adventures that lay ahead. She was eager to immerse herself in the vibrant energy of this bustling metropolis and uncover the poignant stories of those who had been sold into slavery. Tusoli set out to explore the rich history and culture of Benin and In her customary fashion, she began her day by wandering through the streets of Cotonou in search of a local guide. After some inquiries, she was directed to Ouidah, a town renowned for its pivotal role in the transatlantic slave trade – precisely what she had been yearning to explore.

The next day, Tusoli arranged for a taxi to take her to Ouidah, a journey of approximately twenty one miles from her hotel. The taxi driver, well-versed in the history of the area, proved to be a valuable resource, offering insights along the way and even helping her find a knowledgeable tour guide upon arrival. Tusoli and her new guide, Silva, sat down for coffee at a quaint café in Ouidah.

"Hello, I'm Silva. Welcome to Ouidah," he greeted warmly.

"Thank you, I'm Tusoli, and I come from Africatown, Alabama, United States," Tusoli replied, taking in the exotic atmosphere.

"So, you make a living by sharing the history of the slave trade, right?" Tusoli asked, intrigued by Silva's profession.

"This is my profession. I come from a lineage of slave captors, and I hope to reconcile with the descendants of those enslaved by sharing the knowledge passed down to me," Silva answered earnestly.

"Slave captors? That's an incredible job you're doing. It's commendable to accept the fact that the slave trade happened and educate others about it, especially in your position," Tusoli responded, admiring Silva's dedication to preserving history.

"You must be a descendant," Silva guessed, his eyes lighting up with curiosity.

"Yes, I am. That's why I'm here, to see if it really happened," Tusoli confirmed, her voice tinged with emotion.

"You have no doubt that it happened, and this is the route that enslaved individuals took before disappearing into the Door of No Return," Silva said, gesturing towards the iconic doorway.

"My lineage can be traced back to Africatown, Alabama, where a man named Abisai was captured by the people of the Dahomey Kingdom here in Benin and taken to the shore where he boarded the last slave ship to come to the US," Tusoli shared, her words carrying the weight of generations past.

"United States, I've met a few people from there, but it's my pleasure to meet the first descendant of the slaves that boarded The Clotilda. I've always wanted to meet one, and here you are," Silva expressed, his voice filled with genuine admiration and respect.

"You know about The Clotilda?" Tusoli asked, surprised, her eyes widening in disbelief.

"Yes, more than you may know. I come from a direct lineage of one of the commanders who led the raid that captured slaves for The Clotilda from a neighboring kingdom. It was a special slave ship," Silva disclosed, his tone somber yet tinged with a hint of regret.

Tusoli had mixed emotions upon hearing this. She was sitting right in front of a direct descendant of those who captured and sold Abisai into slavery.

"Your forefathers changed our history forever," Tusoli stated with a pang of sadness in her voice, her gaze fixed on Silva.

"I don't understand why they did that, selling their own into torture away from their villages. It breaks my heart every time I share this history, but I am reminded that it must be told boldly to all who seek it. Forgive us for what was done to your people," Silva apologized, his words heavy with remorse.

"I have nothing against you. I'm just seeking knowledge and trying to understand how I ended up in America. I'm glad I met you," Tusoli responded, her tone softening with understanding.

"I will tell you everything. I will show you how it began and where it ended. Be my guest," Silva offered warmly.

"Where do we begin?" Tusoli asked, her curiosity piqued.

"How about we start where it all began, where your forefather was captured?" Silva suggested.

"I would be glad to listen," Tusoli agreed, leaning in attentively.

Silva positioned himself and narrated, "Under the rule of King Ghezo, the economy of Dahomey thrived on the practice of raiding neighboring towns to capture and sell human beings as slaves to European and American traders. Countless individuals were taken captive and transported to the capital of Abomey before being brought to Ouidah for sale. One such trader was a white man who had come to see the King of Dahomey in order to acquire slaves. After a successful transaction, the prince led him to a warehouse where many of the enslaved individuals were kept confined and naked. The man is believed to have chosen one hundred and twenty five slaves, who were then marched to the shore in shackles and transferred by small boats to the waiting ship. Most of them were successfully loaded onto The Clotilda, while some chose to jump overboard into the rough waters rather than face the uncertainty that awaited them onboard."

"The white man was called Captain William Foster," Tusoli recounted. "He was hired by a wealthy shipbuilder in Alabama named Timothy Meaher to come here and buy slaves. According to my mother's account, one hundred and ten slaves arrived in Alabama aboard The Clotilda."

"Wow, I didn't know that part of the story," Silva responded. "I have learned a new piece of history today."

"So where did the slaves wait?" Tusoli inquired.

"We call it the Door of No Return," Silva explained. "It's just a walking distance from here through the Slave Route. Let's go and have a look."

They began their journey on a path winding through the lush and tropical landscapes of Ouidah. Monuments to the strength and resilience of the African people dotted the way. Stone pillars marked the path of the former slave trade, and sculptures depicted crucial moments in African history.

Amidst their walk, Tusoli's eyes caught sight of a large statue of a mother and child standing tall, a poignant symbol of broken families and lost generations. Benches and pathways lined the park, inviting visitors to pause, reflect, and remember. But despite the pain and sorrow of the past, The Slave Route was not merely a path of mourning and loss; it was also a symbol of hope and resilience, celebrating the strength and courage of the African people. It served as a reminder that even in the face of the greatest challenges, it was possible to rise above and forge a brighter future.

It was a place of pilgrimage, healing, and hope—a journey through time that transported us from the depths of the past to the heights of the present. It reminded us that despite our progress, there is still much to be done to create a fairer, more just world for all.

As Tusoli and Silva walked approximately five miles towards the sea, they reached the end of the path, where a monumental arch with murals awaited them on the beach. It was known as The Door of No Return, a solemn tribute to the victims of the slave trade.

The Door of no Return

The Door of No Return, majestic and grand,
Stands solitary by the sea's endless span,
Its weathered stone and rusted brass tell,
Of a past hidden, where heroes fell.
It bears the weight of centuries gone,

Ships came empty, but left full by dawn,
With souls and dreams, forever changed,
By the cruel winds of fate estranged.
It echoes with the cries of the enslaved,
Their tears, their fears, in murals engraved,
Facing a fate so cruel, yet bold,
Their stories of resilience stay untold.
But still it stands, a sentinel of the past,
A portal to memories, shadows cast,
A gateway to a future yet to unfold,
A promise of hope, in stories untold.
For though it marks a tragic plight,
The Door of No Return, in fading light,
Holds the promise of a brighter day,
For those who seek to find their way.
It beckons with a whisper, soft and clear,
To tread the soil of ancestors near,
To feel their spirit, to share their pain,
And honor their legacy, again and again.

CHAPTER 18
DOOR OF NO RETURN, OUIDAH

The "Door of No Return" is a term used to describe the final departure point for millions of African people who were enslaved and forcibly taken from their homes in West Africa during the transatlantic slave trade. Located in Ouidah, Benin, this door marked the last place where enslaved individuals would see their homeland before being transported to the Americas and the Caribbean to endure a life of slavery. It serves as a solemn reminder of the brutal and inhumane history of the transatlantic slave trade, where families were torn apart, individuals were stripped of their freedom, and countless lives were lost to the horrors of slavery.

The Door of No Return stands as a powerful symbol of the transatlantic slave trade, with its murals and sculptures vividly recounting the harrowing journey of millions of Africans torn from their homes and thrust into slavery. Engraved murals depict scenes of enslaved men and women marching towards the sea, the awaiting ship, and the distant tree, each image evoking the profound pain and trauma inflicted by the slave trade.

The sculptures on either side of the arch, portraying enslaved Africans in chains, stand as solemn reminders of the brutal realities of slavery and the injustices inflicted upon them. Among them, the presence of the Egungun figure, representing the spirits of departed ancestors, underscores the deep cultural roots of these enslaved individuals and their enduring connection to their homeland.

In essence, the Door of No Return stands as a powerful memorial to the transatlantic slave trade and a testament to the resilience and strength of the

African people who endured this brutal chapter of history. Visiting the Door of No Return allows people to gain a deeper understanding of the history of slavery and its enduring impact. It offers an opportunity to honor the memories of the millions of enslaved Africans who suffered and perished as a result of this cruel and inhumane system.

Tusoli stood in front of the massive arch, feeling overwhelmed by the weight of its history. The Door of No Return was not just a memorial; it was a symbol of the atrocities committed against millions of Africans. As she gazed upon the images etched into the stone, she couldn't help but imagine the fear and heartbreak that must have consumed the enslaved men and women as they walked toward the waiting ships. The bronze sculptures at either side of the arch depicted enslaved Africans in chains, staring out at the sea, their faces conveying the profound sadness, fear, and loss they must have felt in that moment. Nearby stood an Egungun, a traditional masked figure representing the ancestors they were leaving behind.

Tusoli felt a tear slide down her cheek as she stood before the massive arch. The Door of No Return loomed over her, its ancient stone etched with tales of sorrow and resilience. It was more than just a monument; it was a portal to a dark chapter in history. She imagined the enslaved Africans, their feet worn from miles of travel, their spirits heavy with the weight of captivity. They stood on this very shore, facing the unknown expanse of the sea, where ships waited to carry them far from their homeland. Some, unable to bear the thought of a life in chains, leaped into the sea, choosing freedom in death over bondage in life.

But others, like Abisai, accepted their fate and stepped onto those vessels, never to return. The Door of No Return marked their final farewell to Africa, a land they would never see again. Yet amidst the sorrow, Tusoli sensed a flicker of hope. For in the faces of those bronze sculptures, she saw not just pain, but also strength and resilience. These were not merely victims; they were survivors, their spirits unbroken despite the chains that bound them.

As she stood there, surrounded by the echoes of the past, Tusoli felt a deep sense of connection to her ancestors. Their struggles were her struggles, their triumphs her triumphs. And in that moment, she knew that their legacy would live on, a testament to the enduring spirit of the African people.

"What a collection of powerful murals," Tusoli whispered, her voice filled with sorrow.

She couldn't help but picture Abisai's journey through the Door of No Return, onto the waiting boats, and finally onto The Clotilda. It was as if she could see it all unfolding before her eyes, right there on the beach where her family's history had changed forever. She stood on the sand, imagining it as the last piece of Africa Abisai had stepped on, and scooped up some as a solemn souvenir.

Taking a deep breath, Tusoli looked out at the vast expanse of the ocean, feeling the weight of centuries of pain and suffering. Closing her eyes, she whispered a prayer, asking for peace and forgiveness for the unspeakable atrocities that had taken place during the slavery chapter. As she opened her eyes, she noticed the sun beginning to set, casting a warm glow on the water. The beauty of the moment helped to ease some of the pain she felt, and she realized that despite the atrocities that had taken place, there was still hope for healing and forgiveness. Turning to Silva, Tusoli expressed her heartfelt gratitude,

"Thank you again, Silva. Your kindness and willingness to share your knowledge, especially coming from the tribe of slave captors, mean so much to me."

Silva smiled warmly. "It's my pleasure, Tusoli. I'm glad I could help you on this journey of discovery."

Tusoli knew she would never forget this experience and the valuable lessons she had learned about her history and the importance of remembering the past. As the sun dipped below the horizon, the two decided to enjoy a sundowner at a restaurant near the Ouidah beach. Silva then surprised Tusoli with an invitation to meet his parents,

"You know, my father has a deep appreciation for the history of slavery," Silva said with a smile. "I think he'll be thrilled to meet a descendant of the last slave ship to the USA."

Tusoli's eyes lit up. "If it's not too far from here, I'd love the chance to learn from him. I want to know as much as I can about my ancestry."

Silva nodded with a smile. "It's only about two miles from here. We can take a taxi. I'll make sure you get there safely."

As they made their way to the taxi, Tusoli was struck by the friendliness of the people around her. She felt like she was home, surrounded by warmth and hospitality. Silva was a well-known figure, and people greeted him with respect and admiration as they walked.

From the beach to their destination, Tusoli couldn't shake the feeling that she was stepping into a living history book. She leaned back in the taxi seat, watching the world go by, but her mind was far away, lost in the echoes of the past. She gazed out the window, imagining the men and women who had made the same journey so many years ago. The journey to their new lives as slaves, taken away from their families, their homes, and everything they had ever known.

The streets passed by in a blur, yet bustling with life as Tusoli's mind was transported back in time, feeling the weight of history with each passing moment. She could almost hear the whispers of the ancestors, urging her to remember, to honor, and to never forget. She looked over at Silva, whose eyes were fixed on the passing scenery, lost in his own thoughts. She could see the weight of history in his gaze, a burden carried not just by him, but by generations before him. It was more than a story; it was a part of his family's legacy. She wondered what it must have been like to grow up with that much weight on his shoulders, the legacy of his ancestors' inflicted suffering.

As the taxi pulled up to a small house surrounded by a lush, tropical garden, Silva's demeanor shifted. He led the way with purpose, and Tusoli followed closely behind. This was the place where she would meet Silva's father, a man deeply connected to the legacy of slavery. The door creaked open, and an elderly man emerged. Silva introduced Tusoli, and the old man's eyes twinkled with delight.

"Welcome, my child," he said, embracing Tusoli. "I am honored to meet a descendant of the last slave ship to the Americas. Come, let us sit and talk."

Tusoli felt a wave of reverence wash over her as they settled into comfortable chairs on the veranda. The old man's presence was reassuring, his voice echoing the weight of generations past. She listened intently as he shared stories of his family's history, recounting the sacrifices and hardships they had endured.

She learned of their resilience and strength, how they had persevered through the darkest of times. His words painted a vivid picture of their struggles and triumphs, and Tusoli felt a deep connection as she absorbed every detail.

The old learned man was intrigued and couldn't believe the coincidence. He smiled warmly and offered her some refreshments,

"It's truly a remarkable coincidence to have a descendant of slaves come to my door," he said. "I have dedicated my life to preserving and educating people about the history of slavery, so I am honored to have you here today."

Tusoli was moved by the hospitality she was receiving and was eager to learn more about the history of slavery from a historian's perspective.

"I would love to hear more of your insights on the history of slavery, sir," she said, looking at Silva's father.

"Of course," he replied. "I have dedicated my life to studying this dark chapter in human history and it would be my pleasure to share my knowledge with you. Where would you like to start?"

And so, Tusoli spent the next hour soaking in the wealth of knowledge and history from Silva's father. She was amazed by his passion and dedication to preserving the stories and memories of those who were affected by slavery. She felt grateful for the opportunity to learn from someone with such expertise and for being welcomed into his home.

"Actually, we are from the Dahomey tribe, and our ancestors prospered from the slave trade. They used to raid villages and capture slaves for the Americas and caribbean. There was high demand for African laborers," narrated Silva's father, his voice heavy with emotion.

"What we did was inhuman. The barbaric treatment that our own people went through is beyond comprehension. They were violently taken from their families, shackled, and marched to the sea never to return again," he added, his eyes misting over at the thought.

Tusoli spoke up, "My ancestors were among those taken from here and brought to the United States as forced labor on *The Clotilda*, the last ship to arrive in the States with slaves on board."

Silva's father nodded, "Clotilda. I have read about it in numerous publications, but never in my wildest dreams did I think I would meet someone from Africatown, a direct descendant of *The Clotilda* to be more precise. Many have come here seeking answers, but *The Clotilda's* history will always hold a special place in the annals of slave history. It speaks for millions of Africans abroad who cannot trace their roots. I hope that her discovery will lead to her preservation in a museum, where her history can be relieved and experienced by people of African descent."

"Back home we all hope that The Clotilda can be lifted from the river's muddy bed and placed somewhere new, where her history can be properly remembered and honored," Tusoli said, her voice filled with passion.

Silva's father smiled warmly, "As a symbol of our tribe's quest for forgiveness and reconciliation, we have prepared a special Yoruba porridge for you. We make this offering every year to the other tribes whose ancestors were captured by Dahomey tribesmen."

Tusoli replied with a smile on her face, "Thank you, this means a lot to me."

She savored the rich and traditional Yoruba porridge, feeling peace wash over her. The thought of meeting descendants of the people who once captured her Abisai, and the opportunity to participate in a reconciliation ceremony with them, filled her with gratitude. Yet as night approached, Tusoli felt the need to return to her hotel.

"Thank you for your kindness. I'm really happy to be here, but I think I should head back to my hotel in Cocanou before it gets too dark," she said with a gentle plea.

Silva's father, however, had other plans. "Why don't you stay a bit longer? We have plenty of room for guests and there's still so much to see and learn here in Ouidah. Don't rush away just yet," the old man offered with a warm smile.

Tusoli was unable to resist the invitation and decided to spend the night. Over a delicious African dinner, she got to know more about Silva and his father, both of whom were accomplished historians in their own right. After a night of rich story-telling, it was time to get some rest. They made their way to Tusoli's room, Silverstone still regaling her with stories of the rich culture and history of the Dahomey tribe. She was in awe of the depth of knowledge he possessed and the passion he had for his heritage. Once they reached her room, Silverstone bid her goodnight and left her to settle in.

Tusoli couldn't help but feel a sense of belonging as she explored the room, surrounded by the artifacts and trinkets of a culture she had come to understand and respect. Eventually, she drifted off to sleep, reflecting on the incredible journey she had been on, from her ancestors being taken captive, to finally standing here in Ouidah with the descendants of their captors.

CHAPTER 19
GOODBYE AFRICA

As dawn broke, Tusoli was greeted by the aroma of a sumptuous breakfast prepared by Silva's mother. The sausages, specially made for her, melted in her mouth, filling her tastebuds with delight. Energized by the delicious meal, Tusoli eagerly accepted Silva's invitation to explore the vibrant Ouidah market and other enchanting sights.

By noon, Tusoli and Silva found themselves by the shimmering shores of Cocanou beach. The rhythmic sound of the waves crashing against the shore provided a soothing backdrop as they settled in for a beachside lunch. Under the shade of a swaying palm tree, they feasted on fresh seafood and tropical fruits, their laughter mingling with the ocean breeze.

"I hope your time here in Ouidah was nothing short of delightful," Silva said with a warm smile.

"It was beyond anything I could've imagined, your family's hospitality was unmatched," Tusoli responded, her eyes shining with gratitude.

Silva then inquired, "Are the wedding bells ringing in Africatown for you?"

Tusoli, taken aback by the question, replied, "No, I am not yet married nor planning to. Why do you ask?"

Silva leaned in, "My father has expressed to me that he has plenty of fertile lands and cattle waiting for you at our home."

Tusoli could hardly believe what she was hearing and chuckled, "For me? Are you serious?"

Silva nodded "Dead serious. You are a radiant and intelligent woman, and my father already sees you as his future daughter-in-law."

Tusoli was left speechless, overwhelmed by the kind gesture, "I'm at a loss for words Silva. Your father's generosity is truly heartwarming."

"I got a scholarship to teach black history in New York and my Visa is almost ready. It would be great to have you in my life as we can explore this history together" Silva added. "Just a random question, would you consider marrying from Africa?" Silva raised a brow.

Tusoli paused to ponder before saying, "I've never thought about it before. I've been traveling the continent to discover my history, but maybe we could dig deeper into this when you come to New York. So, you'd better come!"

Silva smiled warmly and said, "Here in Ouidah, we believe in traditional matchmaking, where the parents of both families come together to make a decision. And my father believes that you would be a perfect match for me."

Tusoli, still taken aback by the sudden proposal, asked, "Really? I had no idea this was even a possibility."

Silva nodded, "Yes, it is, and I would be honored to have you as my wife. I have seen the beauty of your character and the kindness in your heart, and I believe that we would make a great team together."

Tusoli thought for a moment and said, "I'm flattered by your offer Silva, but I need to think about it. Can I have some time to consider it?"

Silva nodded understandingly and said, "Of course, take all the time you need. I understand that this is a big decision."

Tusoli was grateful for the offer and the opportunity to experience this unique culture. She knew that this decision would impact the rest of her life, but she was willing to explore this possibility and see where it would take her. She thanked Silva for his kindness and understanding, and promised to keep him updated on her decision.

Silva's grin broadened, "Your ride is here." He turned and gestured to a waiting car. "It was a pleasure."

Tusoli agreed, "The pleasure was mine. Keep my number safe and call me when you come to New York. I want to return the kindness you've shown me."

It was then that Silva approached her, holding a chain in his hand. "Have this, Tusoli," he said. "It means a lot in my culture, made of shells from the sea. It will always bring you good luck. May I help you put it on?."

With a smile, Tusoli accepted the gift with gratitude as Silva helped her fasten the chain around her neck.

He then took Tusoli's hand and said, "Goodbye, Tusoli. I hope to see you soon." He held her gaze, a promise of adventure and discovery shining in his eyes.

Tusoli departed Ouidah with a profound sense of closure, feeling as though she had come full circle. She had embarked on a journey that honored her ancestors and their memories, and now, as she left the city behind, she carried their legacy with her. The haunting image of the Door of No Return remained etched in her mind, serving as a poignant reminder of the impact Africa had on her life.

Tusoli realized the significance of her travels. Her path had led her back to where it all began, to right where The Clotilda bought her people, changing the course of history forever. It was a moment of profound realization for Tusoli—a journey of self-discovery and a deep connection to her roots, completing a full circle that spanned generations. With a heart full of gratitude and a renewed sense of identity, she looked forward to the next chapter of her life with a newfound sense of purpose.

As the taxi pulled away from the Door of No Return monument in Ouidah, she gazed back at the slowly disappearing arch, and was transported back in time to the moment when Abisai, along with many others, was forced to embark on a one-way journey to the Americas. She envisioned Abisai's last steps on African soil as he waded into the small boat, his eyes fixed on the endless horizon and his heart heavy with sorrow. But as she touched the chain that hung around her neck, Tusoli felt a sense of accomplishment and forgiveness.

Having grappled with the haunting legacy of slavery, Tusoli now found herself reconciled and at peace as she prepared to depart the continent. The chain around her neck, once a heavy reminder of history's weight, now carried a new significance. Through her journey, she had forged reconciliation with the past and a profound connection to the events of slavery. It had been a cathartic experience, drawing her closer to her roots and providing the closure she had long sought.

With her time in Africa drawing to a close, Tusoli realized that it marked not an end, but the beginning of a lifelong bond with the continent that would forever shape her existence. Returning to her hotel in Coconou, she prepared to conclude her journey, packing her bags and finalizing her arrangements for the journey back home. The anticipation of reuniting with her eagerly awaiting mother after six long weeks filled her with a mix of excitement and longing.

Reflecting on her African odyssey, Tusoli understood that while her physical journey was ending, the memories and lessons she had amassed would endure. Each experience had become a part of her, intricately woven into the chain around her neck. She had searched deep into her own identity and history, and now felt compelled to share this newfound knowledge with future generations, eager to perpetuate the legacy of her journey for years to come.

The following day, in the afternoon, her taxi picked her up with all her luggage and headed for the Airport. She did all the checks and in no time, she was sitting in the plane ready for take-off. Eventually the plane was in the skies of Benin taking her back home; though she felt she was actually leaving home. She stared blankly through the window above the clouds reminiscing every moment she's had in Africa. As the plane gained altitude, Tusoli felt a pang of sadness in her heart. She was leaving behind a place that had come to mean so much to her, a place where she had connected with her roots and discovered a new sense of identity. She closed her eyes and took a deep breath, feeling grateful for the journey and the experiences she had gained.

She then gazed out the window of the plane and all she could see was the endless expanse of the continent below her, realizing that she had only just scratched the surface of its rich and vibrant culture. She made a promise to herself to return soon, to explore even more of the land of her ancestors and to continue her journey of self-discovery. She knew that Africa would always hold a special place in her heart.

After many hours in the skies, Tusoli's sleep was interrupted as the captain's voice filled the cabin, announcing their descent into the city of New York. The plane began to make its way through the clouds and Tusoli could see the sprawling cityscape slowly coming into view. Excitement mixed with nervousness filled her as she realized that the journey was coming to an end. As she stepped off the plane and into the busy airport terminal, she felt a wave of emotions wash over her.

Her journey had come to an end. She hugged her luggage close and made her way out of the airport, eager to be reunited with her family and share with them all that she had learned and experienced. The chain hanging from her neck felt heavy with the memories she had made, but also light with the knowledge that this was only the beginning of a new chapter in her life. With her luggage in tow, she made her way to the next gate, eagerly anticipating her next flight to Atlanta, Georgia.

Tusoli finally arrived in Atlanta. She stepped into the waiting area, her eyes scanning the sea of faces, searching for one in particular. And there he was, Pete, standing tall and proud, with a beaming smile on his face.

The sight of him was enough to send Tusoli into a frenzied sprint, her arms outstretched as she raced towards him. With a joyful cry, she threw herself into Pete's waiting arms, hugging him tightly as if she would never let go. Her excitement was contagious, as Pete's smile grew even wider, his eyes shining with happiness at the reunion. It was clear they had truly missed each other.

"Look at you, I've missed you! It feels like ages have passed," said Pete.

"I've missed you too, Pete. You look different, you look great. What have you been up to?" Tusoli replied.

"Just taking care of myself and staying out of trouble. I missed you," Pete replied with a chuckle.

Tusoli noticed that Pete had made some changes. He was more muscular and the suit he was wearing gave him an executive appearance. Pete picked up her luggage and they walked to the waiting car.

"I thought you were with my mother," Tusoli asked.

"The bakery has been so busy, so I thought it would be best if I came to pick you up alone. We can stop by the bakery before I drop you both off at home," Pete explained.

He opened the car door for Tusoli and put her luggage in the trunk before starting the engine. They then set off for Auburn.

"You must be exhausted," Pete said.

"I am so tired. I can't wait to see my mother," Tusoli replied.

"She'll be thrilled to see you," Pete added.

"So, how was your time in Africa?" Pete asked.

"It was nothing short of incredible, Pete. I loved every moment of it. I've learned so much and Africa is truly beautiful," Tusoli replied.

"Do you plan on going back there?" Pete asked while driving to exit the airport.

"Definitely, there's still so much I want to see and experience," Tusoli said.

"What's next for you, now that you are back?" Pete asked.

"I haven't decided yet. I might take care of my grandfather's estate or help my mother with the bakery. But I'm also considering setting up a healthcare humanitarian organization in Kenya or Benin. I'm still considering my options," Tusoli said.

Pete then shifted the conversation in a surprising direction. "It seems like Africa has captured your heart. How about we begin a new chapter there, just the two of us?" Pete proposed.

"You and me? Are you suggesting we go to Africa together?" Tusoli asked, taken aback.

"Yes, exactly. I've been waiting for you to return so we could have this conversation. I love you, Tusoli, and I envision us building a new life, perhaps in Africa," Pete confessed.

"I know how you feel about me, Pete, and I can't deny that I have feelings for you too. But let's take things slow and see where it goes," Tusoli replied cautiously.

"I want you to be mine, Tusoli. Let me reveal another side of myself to you, one you've never seen before. Let me be the man you've always deserved," Pete pleaded.

"I need some time to consider it, Pete. Can we revisit this discussion after we've settled back in Auburn?" Tusoli requested.

"Of course. Take all the time you need," Pete assured her, his tone softening.

When they finally arrived in Auburn, Tusoli couldn't wait to reunite with her mother at the bakery. The two women embraced tightly, their joy palpable as they caught up on missed moments. Tusoli marveled at how much the business had flourished in just two months, her heart swelling with pride for her mother's success. As they sat down to enjoy a special cake shaped like Africa, prepared especially for her by Helena, Tusoli couldn't help but beam with delight. With each bite, she savored not only the sweetness of the cake but also the warmth of family and the richness of her heritage.

"This is the tastiest cake I've ever had, Mom. What do you think, Pete?" Tusoli inquired eagerly.

"I'm at a loss for words. It's incredibly delicious. Well done, Helena," Pete complimented with a smile.

"Thank you, dear ones. I'm delighted you both enjoyed it," Helena replied graciously. After a delightful afternoon catching up and savoring the cake, they bid farewell and headed home. Tusoli was eager to rest and recover from the effects of the jet lag.

One early morning, Tusoli's phone rang, the ringtone echoing through the quiet room like a distant drumbeat. With a flutter of excitement, she answered, already knowing who it would be.

"Silva, it's so good to hear from you!" She exclaimed, her voice filled with anticipation.

"Oh, sorry, it's actually Leonardo," came the reply, his voice a surprising twist in the conversation. "I just wanted to check in and see how you're doing."

Tusoli's heart skipped a beat, momentarily disappointed, but she quickly recovered, still happy to hear from her friend.

"Leonardo, I thought you were back in Atlanta. I left Africa and am now in Alabama," she said, a hint of surprise in her tone.

"I've been traveling and experiencing new places, but I'll be in Georgia next week," Leonardo said, his voice filled with excitement. "I can't wait to come visit you in Auburn."

Tusoli's face lit up with a smile. "You're always welcome, Leonardo. Just let me know when you arrive. Stay safe on your journey," she said, hanging up the phone.

Tusoli then headed to the bakery to help his mother with the day's orders. But as she was arranging the baked goods, she froze as Jonathan stepped in, his presence casting a shadow over the room.

"Hey Tusoli, I see you're back in town. How are you?" Jonathan said, his voice dripping with false cheer.

Helena, sensing the tension thickening the air, intervened. "Jonathan never went to jail, and Rudolph is devastated. Why don't you two talk outside?"

With a silent nod, Tusoli reluctantly followed Jonathan outside to a nearby cafe.

"You should be in jail, Jonathan," Tusoli said, her voice shaking with anger.

"I never killed Karina, Tusoli," Jonathan replied, his eyes downcast.

"What do you mean? Who killed her?" Tusoli asked, her mind racing.

"It was an accident. Karina fell and hit her head on the sink. I tried to save her, but she passed away in the emergency room," Jonathan explained, his voice cracking.

"But we all know the truth Jonathan. You pushed her," Tusoli accused, her fists clenched.

"I was scared and confused. I'm not a murderer, Tusoli. I didn't kill Karina," Jonathan protested, his eyes pleading for understanding.

Tusoli didn't know what to think. All she knew was that she couldn't trust Jonathan, not after everything that had happened. "I'm sorry, Jonathan, but I can't believe you," she said, her heart heavy with sadness.

Jonathan begged, "I understand why you wouldn't believe me, but I swear I am telling the truth. I loved Karina, I would never harm her. I just panicked when I saw her fall and I couldn't think straight. I made a huge mistake, but I couldn't bear the thought of spending my life in prison for something I didn't do. Please Tusoli, you have to believe me."

Tusoli was torn. On one hand, she had known Jonathan for years and he had never given her any reason to suspect he was capable of such a terrible act. On the other hand, she had seen the police report and the evidence seemed to point towards his guilt. She needed more time to think things over and decide what to do.

"Jonathan, I don't know what to believe right now. I need time to process this information and figure out what the truth is. Can we talk again in a few days?" Tusoli asked.

Jonathan nodded in agreement, "Take all the time you need Tusoli. I just hope you can see that I am telling the truth."

Tusoli's mind was racing with conflicting thoughts and emotions. She felt like she needed to find a way to get to the bottom of this and figure out what really happened to Karina.

As Jonathan spoke, his words hung in the air, heavy with the weight of his confession, "I am planning to leave Alabama, go to some other city Maybe New York or just some place far away. I want you to know that I never stopped loving you. My heart still feels the same way. I can take you with me and we can forget about the past and make a new beginning"

Tusoli answered him, "I'm sorry, Jonathan. My heart just isn't ready to forgive and forget. I still need time to heal from the past and what you did."

Jonathan gave a deep sigh, "I understand. But just remember, my love for you will never fade. And if you ever change your mind, I'll be waiting."

They shared a heart-wrenching embrace before she eventually parted ways with him. The encounter left Tusoli disturbed, unable to shake off the memory of their time together. With that, Jonathan left the cafe and disappeared into the crowd. Tusoli watched him go, her heart torn between the love she once had for him and the pain he caused. She returned to the bakery, but her mind was consumed by thoughts of Jonathan and the past they shared. The rest of the evening was a blur as she tried to come to terms with her feelings. Would she ever be able to move on and start a new chapter in her life? Only time would tell.

Tusoli couldn't shake off the feelings she had when she was in Jonathan's arms. She knew that she shouldn't be thinking about him and that she should focus on moving forward with her life, but she couldn't help it. She couldn't deny the fact that she still had feelings for him, even after everything that had happened. She was so lost in thought that she didn't even hear her mother calling her name.

"Tusoli, Tusoli! Where are you?"

"Oh, sorry mom. I was just thinking," she replied.

"About what?" her mother asked.

"Jonathan?" Her mother sighed.

"Tusoli, you can't keep dwelling on the past. You have to move on and make a new future for yourself. Jonathan is not good for you, he has caused you so much pain. You deserve better than that."

Tusoli knew that her mother was right. She needed to focus on herself and not on the past. So she promised herself that she would not let Jonathan consume her thoughts anymore and that she would focus on building a new life for herself.

"Mom, why didn't you tell me Jonathan was released?" Tusoli asked.

"The police said they didn't have enough evidence to convict him of murder," Helena replied. "Rudolph did his best to get justice for Karina, but there just wasn't enough proof."

Tusoli pondered, "Do you think Jonathan's father had something to do with it, he could have used his influence?"

"With his release? It's possible, but it's a complicated case," Helena said.

Tusoli wondered, "Do you believe he killed Karina?"

"What was he saying to you out there? Trying to convince you of his innocence?" Helena asked. "Do you not remember how much he hurt you?"

"I don't know what to think, Mom," Tusoli said. "What if it was just an accident, like he says?"

Helena was shocked, "Are you still in love with that lunatic? Please tell me you're not. I don't want to ever see you near that boy again."

Tusoli tried to explain, "Just hear me out, Mom. It could have just been a freak accident. Think about it"

"Are you listening to yourself? That boy got your best friend pregnant, forced her to abort and then he killed her, whether an accident or not, he caused her death, and you want me to think about it?

You're not making sense, Tusoli. We're not having this conversation anymore. Goodnight."

The next few months were a tumultuous time for Tusoli. On one hand, there was Silva, the handsome suitor from Africa who had traveled from Benin to Georgia to ask for her hand in marriage. He arrived with the blessings of his father and a heart overflowing with love and devotion.

On the other hand, there was Leonardo, a persistent admirer who refused to be deterred by distance. He spent three intense days in Auburn, pouring his heart out and declaring his undying love for Tusoli.

And then there was Pete, her steadfast friend and confidante, who longed to be her Romeo and sweep her off her feet.

Then, there was Jonathan, the one who still held a smoldering flame in her heart, hoping for a chance to reignite the ruins of their love.

In the midst of all these suitors, Tusoli found herself torn and confused, facing the difficult decision of choosing one to spend the rest of her life with. After days of pondering deeply, her mind was constantly plagued with doubts and questions about the past. Was Jonathan truly innocent in Karina's death or was he just trying to convince her? Could she really trust Leonardo and his intentions towards her? What about Pete, was she ready to break the friendship boundaries? Was Silva a good match for her, would it bring reconciliation over her history? It was a difficult time for Tusoli as she struggled to make a decision that would determine her future.

One evening, consumed by an inner turmoil she could no longer ignore, Tusoli made a decision. She couldn't shake the memories of Jonathan, the weight of his words, the depth of their shared history. With resolve in her heart, she found herself standing outside Jonathan's small apartment on the outskirts of Auburn. He welcomed her inside and as she entered, Tusoli was a little shocked. Jonathan, once vibrant and full of life, now sat slouched on a worn-out couch, a shadow of his former self. His eyes, once filled with confidence, now bore the weight of guilt and regret.

Sitting across from him, Tusoli couldn't help but notice the change in him. He was no longer the carefree young man she once knew. He was broken, haunted by his own demons, a stark contrast to the Jonathan she remembered.

"Jonathan, why did you really come to Auburn?" she asked calmly.

"I came because I wanted to tell you the truth," he replied,

"I never stopped loving you, Tusoli," Jonathan's voice was raw, his eyes pleading as he spoke. "And I couldn't move on knowing that you thought I was capable of murder. Without you in my life, I feel like it's just the end of the world." Each word carried the weight of his emotions, echoing in the quiet room like a solemn vow.

Tusoli listened intently as Jonathan recounted his side of the story, his words painting a picture of a tragic accident and the overwhelming guilt that had consumed him since. With each detail he shared, Tusoli felt her heart soften, realizing she had been too quick to judge and too harsh on him.

A sense of compassion welled up inside her as she saw the pain etched in Jonathan's eyes, a stark contrast to the anger she had felt towards him. She felt a deep sadness for what he had been through, understanding now the heavy burden he had been carrying alone.

One year later, after much contemplation and consideration, Tusoli had finally made her choice. And in a grand celebration filled with love, laughter, and tears of joy, she exchanged vows with the one who had captured her heart.

The wedding was a grand affair, held in the quaint and picturesque town of Auburn. The air was filled with anticipation and excitement as family, friends, and well-wishers gathered to witness the union of two souls.

Amidst the backdrop of blooming flowers and the soft glow of candlelight, Tusoli and Peterson McGreg declared their love for each other in front of all those who mattered most. It was a day that would be forever etched in the annals of time, as the day when Tusoli found her happily ever after.

My happily ever after
Oh love, the luckiest man I be
To find a gem so bright and fair
A human full of grace and glee
With charm and presence beyond compare.
Your humor shines like summer sun
Right and wrong, you always know
Your taste is cultured, mind so wise
With chivalry that never grows old.
In every life, in every time
My love for you, it will remain
A choice I made, this ring's a sign
Of our love, in sickness and in health.

This fabric of human skin, so fine
Is all I need, to call mine
Together we'll embark on life's quest
With love as our eternal nest.
Beating heart, this gentle soul
This mind so wise and full of grace
I am grateful for you every day,
For you complete my every space.
With this ring I marry you
And vow to stand by your side
Through every joy, every trial,
Through every moment by your side.
So here's to love, and laughter,
To dreams that we will share,
To a future bright with happiness,
With you, my love, right there.
You are my best friend, my partner,
The one who makes my life complete,
And I promise you this day, my love,
That I will always love and keep.
Your sparkling eyes and radiant smile
Your warm embrace, your gentle touch
Have made my life so much worthwhile
I am grateful for you so much.
You are my better half, my soulmate
Together, our love will never fade
I promise to be there for you, always
To love and cherish you, till the end of days.
With this ring, I pledge my love
To be yours forever and always
To walk hand in hand, through life's journey
And face all its challenges with grace.
So today, I marry you with all my heart
In front of our friends and family
Together, let us start a new chapter

Of love, happiness, and unity.

The newlyweds made a solemn vow to honor and preserve the legacy of those who were enslaved on *The Clotilda*. They recognized the importance of educating future generations about the atrocities of slavery and committed themselves to ensuring that the story of *The Clotilda* is never forgotten. They also pledged to fight for equality and justice for all, and to work towards creating a world where no one is oppressed or discriminated against based on their race or ethnicity. And lastly, they made a promise to advocate for *The Clotilda* to be properly recognized and given a permanent home above the murky waters of the Mobile River, where it would serve as a powerful symbol of the resilience and strength of those who survived the horrors of slavery.

Following their honeymoon exploring the magnificent pyramids of Giza in Egypt, from the majestic Sphinx guarding the plateau to the vibrant hustle and bustle of Cairo's markets, the couple returned to Auburn and arranged to attend *The Clotilda's* third anniversary since its discovery.

When the day finally came for The Clotilda's discovery anniversary, the two, together with Helena, drove to Africatown eager to meet other community members and forge the way forward. Upon arrival at the community center, they were greeted by familiar faces, including Rudolph. The room was packed with friends and locals, all eager to listen and share their thoughts. The meeting was held at the community center in Africatown.

People from all walks of life, young and old, came together to discuss the fate of *The Clotilda*, the last known slave ship to bring Africans to the United States. As the gathering began, a gentleman welcomed everyone and said a prayer before inviting the community chairman to give his speech. The room was filled with an air of anticipation as the community leaders addressed the gathering. The discussions centered around the need to raise the shipwreck from the muddy Mobile River bed, where it had been resting for over a century.

"We are gathered here today to talk about our history and the history of *The Clotilda,* the ship that was once the last bastion of slavery in America," began the community chairman.

The people listened with rapt attention as he went on to explain the significance of *The Clotilda* in their history. He talked about the bravery and resilience of their ancestors who had survived the horrors of slavery and went on to create a thriving community in Africatown.

"But our history is under threat. *The Clotilda,* the last remaining symbol of our struggle, is lying in the riverbed, slowly deteriorating, and we must act now to preserve it," he said.

The community leaders called for a plan of action to raise *The Clotilda* from the riverbed and to establish a museum to house it. They argued that the ship was a vital piece of African-American history and its preservation was important for future generations. The meeting was heated, with emotions running high as people shared their opinions and concerns. Some felt that the cost of raising the ship was too high, while others argued that *The Clotilda* was an essential part of their heritage and its preservation was worth any cost.

Hours ticked by with heated discussions and debates. The community leader had a surprise in store for the gathering. He rose to his feet and said, "I would like to invite a special guest to speak with us today. Most of you know her mother Helena. She is one of us, and has a unique perspective on the history we are discussing. Please help me in welcoming Tusoli Tolewa."

The room erupted into a thunderous round of applause as Tusoli made her way to the front of the room. She took a deep breath to gather her thoughts. She gazed around the room at the faces of the people she had known all her life. They were here, in this hall in Africatown, to discuss the future of *The Clotilda* and their history as descendants of slaves brought over on that ship.

"Thank you all for having me here today," she began. "As some of you may know, I recently traveled to Africa and visited the very place where *The Clotilda* bought slaves from the Dahomey Kingdom. It was a deeply emotional experience for me, as I was able to see firsthand the atrocities that were committed against our ancestors."

The room fell silent as Tusoli continued to speak, her voice growing stronger with each passing word. She shared stories of the people she met in Africa, of their resilience and strength in the face of unimaginable hardship. She spoke of the importance of preserving the history of slavery and ensuring that future generations never forget the struggles of their ancestors.

"Brothers and sisters, I traveled there to trace the steps of our ancestors who were taken from their homes and brought to America on *The Clotilda*."

The room was silent as everyone listened intently to Tusoli's unique story.

"I stood on the shores of the Ocean where *The Clotilda* was docked, and I felt the weight of history on my shoulders. I imagined the horror that my ancestors must have felt as they were taken from their homes and loaded onto that ship."

Tusoli paused for a moment to collect her thoughts before continuing.

"I saw the poverty and despair that still exists in that part of Africa today. It is a stark reminder of the devastation that the slave trade caused to our people. And yet, even in the face of that suffering, there is hope. There is hope that we can preserve the memory of our ancestors and honor their legacy by raising *The Clotilda* from the muddy Mobile Riverbed and placing it in a museum."

The room erupted in applause and shouts of agreement. Tusoli had touched a nerve with her passionate plea for the preservation of history.

"My fellow community members," she added. "I saw the ruins of the slave forts where they were held captive before being shipped across the ocean, and like I said, I stood in the same spot where *The Clotilda* bought the last group of slaves ever to be brought to America. And I am here to tell you, my friends, that we cannot let *The Clotilda* remain at the bottom of that muddy riverbed."

There were murmurs of agreement from the group. Tusoli knew that they all understood the significance of the Clotilda and what it represented to their community.

"That ship is not just a relic of the past," Tusoli continued. "It is a symbol of our ancestors' struggle, their resilience, and their triumph over oppression. It represents our history, our heritage, and our identity as a people. And we cannot allow it to be forgotten, to be lost in the murky depths of the Mobile River."

"As a community, we must come together and demand that *The Clotilda* be brought up from the depths of the river and given the respect it deserves. Our ancestors suffered unimaginable horrors on that ship, and it is our duty to ensure that their story is never forgotten."

The room erupted in applause and shouts of agreement.

"But what can we do?" one person asked.

"We can start by bringing attention to *The Clotilda* and its importance to our community," Tusoli replied.

"We can tell our story to the world, share our history and culture, and demand that *The Clotilda* be raised from the riverbed and be preserved in a museum for generations to come."

There were more nods and murmurs of agreement. Tusoli could see that her message was being received loud and clear.

"This is just the beginning," she said, her voice rising. "We have a long road ahead of us, but I know that we can do this. We can honor our ancestors, preserve our history, and ensure that our children and grandchildren know their roots. We can fight for justice and equality, and we can make a difference in this world. Are you with me?"

The room erupted in cheers and applause, the people on their feet, fists raised in solidarity. Tusoli smiled, her heart filled with pride and hope. They had a long way to go, but together, they could achieve anything.

"And that is why I believe it is so important that we work to raise the Clotilda from the muddy riverbed and preserve it in a museum," Tusoli concluded.

"It is a symbol of our history, a reminder of the pain and suffering that our ancestors endured. But it is also a testament to their strength and resilience, and a symbol of hope for the future."

The room erupted into applause as Tusoli finished speaking, and the community leader stood up to address the gathering once again.

"Thank you, Tusoli, for sharing your story with us today," he said. "You have reminded us of the importance of our history and the need to preserve it for future generations. Let us continue to work together to ensure that *The Clotilda* is raised from the riverbed and given the respect it deserves."

Tusoli's words hung in the air as the meeting came to a close. The community members left the room with a renewed sense of purpose, ready to fight for the preservation of their history and the memory of their ancestors.

Oh Clotilda

Oh Clotilda, long lost ship of pain,
Buried in mud, hidden from sight again,
Your story, a testament to the past,
A reminder of a time that cannot last.
Your wooden planks, once carried the weight,
Of human bodies, trapped in a terrible fate,
Sold and traded, across the seas,
Forced to suffer, on bended knees.
Oh Clotilda, your legacy must live on,
In a place where your story will never be gone,
A museum, a home, where all can learn,
Of the horrors of slavery, and how we must turn.
Let your rusted hull, now be raised,
From the riverbed, where you were once misplaced,
And let the world see, the evidence of our past,
So we may learn, and never repeat it again, at last.
Oh Clotilda, may you rest in peace,
In a place where your story will never cease,
A reminder of the wrongs we must right,
So we may live in a world that's truly bright.

FM. NICKSON

THE END

HISTORY OF THE DOOR OF NO RETURN

The Door of No Return is a term that is widely used to describe the last portal that African slaves passed through before being forced to board ships and sent to the New World. The door was located in several West African countries, including Ghana, Senegal, and Benin, and was a key symbol of the slave trade that operated from the 16th to the 19th centuries. It represented the final goodbye to Africa for the many slaves that were captured and sold into slavery. The door became a powerful symbol of the horrors of the slave trade and the suffering that African people were subjected to during this dark period of history. In this brief article, we will explore the history and significance of the Door of No Return.

The History of the Door of No Return

The history of the Door of No Return is closely tied to the history of the slave trade in West Africa. The slave trade began in the 16th century when European traders began to sail to the African continent to buy slaves. The trade was driven by the demand for labor in the European colonies in the New World, particularly in the Caribbean and South America. Slaves were captured from various African countries, including Ghana, Senegal, and Benin, and were forced to march long distances to the coast. Many died on the way due to starvation, dehydration, or disease. Those who survived were taken to forts on the coast, where they were held until they could be loaded onto ships and sent across the Atlantic to the New World. The Door of No Return was the final step in this process. Slaves were led through the door and onto the waiting ships that would take them to their new lives in the Americas. For many, this was a journey from which they would never return.

The Door of No Return in Ghana

The Door of No Return in Ghana is perhaps the most famous of all the doors. It is located in the Cape Coast Castle, a fort that was built by the British in the late 17th century. The fort was one of the largest in West Africa and was used to hold slaves before they were loaded onto ships and sent to the New World. The Door of No Return in the Cape Coast Castle was a small opening that led directly onto the beach. Slaves were forced to walk through the door and onto the waiting ships that were anchored just offshore. They were packed into the ships like sardines, often with little or no room to move. The journey across the Atlantic was long and grueling, and many died before they reached their destination. Today, the Cape Coast Castle is a popular tourist destination, and the Door of No Return is a poignant reminder of the horrors of the slave trade. Visitors can walk through the door and onto the beach, imagining what it must have been like for the thousands of slaves who passed through the same opening before them.

The Door of No Return in Senegal

The Door of No Return in Senegal is located on Goree Island, just off the coast of Dakar. Goree Island was a major center of the slave trade in West Africa and was home to several forts and trading posts. The island was a key stopping point for slaves on their way to the New World, and the Door of No Return was the final step in the process. The Door of No Return on Goree Island is a small opening that leads directly onto the beach. Slaves were forced to walk through the door and onto the waiting ships that were anchored just offshore. The journey across the Atlantic was long and arduous, and many died before they reached their destination. Today, Goree Island is a popular tourist destination, and the Door of No Return is a powerful symbol of the suffering that African slaves endured during the slave trade. Visitors can walk through the door and onto the beach, experiencing a small fraction of what the slaves must have felt when they were forced to pass through the same opening.

The Door of No Return in Benin

The Door of No Return in Benin is located in the city of Ouidah, which was a major center of the slave trade in West Africa. The city was home to several forts and trading posts, and slaves were often held in these forts before they were loaded onto ships and sent to the New World. The Door of No Return in Ouidah is a large arch that was built in the 1990s to commemorate the slaves who passed through the city on their way to the New World. The arch is located on the beach and is a powerful symbol of the suffering that African slaves endured during the slave trade. Today, Ouidah is a popular tourist destination, and the Door of No Return is a poignant reminder of the horrors of the slave trade. Visitors can walk through the arch and onto the beach, experiencing a small part of what the slaves must have felt when they were forced to pass through the same city on their way to a life of slavery.

The Significance of the Door of No Return

The Door of No Return is a powerful symbol of the suffering that African slaves endured during the slave trade. For many, passing through the door meant leaving their families and communities behind forever, and beginning a life of forced labor and servitude in a foreign land. It is also a symbol of resistance and resilience. Despite the horrors of the slave trade, African people never gave up their fight for freedom and dignity. The legacy of the Door of No Return is a testament to the strength and courage of African people in the face of oppression and adversity. Today, the Door of No Return is a reminder of the need for continued vigilance against the forces of oppression and injustice. The legacy of the slave trade is still with us today, in the form of racism, economic inequality, and other forms of discrimination. The Door of No Return serves as a powerful symbol of the struggle for freedom and equality that must continue to be fought in every corner of the world. It is a powerful symbol of the horrors of the slave trade and the suffering that African people endured during this dark period of history. The door represented the final goodbye to Africa for many slaves, and it was a stark reminder of the injustice and oppression that they would face in the New World. Today, the Door of No Return is a reminder of the need to continue the struggle for freedom and equality. The legacy of the slave trade is still with us today, and it must be confronted and overcome if we are to build a world that is truly just and equitable for all. The Door of No Return serves as a powerful symbol of the struggle for a better future, and it will continue to inspire generations to come.

From the Author,

3050

The world is a shadow of its former self, a testament to the catastrophic event that ravaged the planet nearly a millennium ago. The aftermath of this disaster can still be felt, with climate change and environmental disasters continuing to wreak havoc on the earth. The once-beautiful natural landscapes have been decimated, and humanity has been forced to retreat into vast, fortified cities that offer some measure of protection against the toxic air, radiation, and blistering sun. "3050" is the gripping tale of a genetically-engineered creature created to defeat a deadly threat to humanity.

WHISPERS OF THE HEART

From the first blush of attraction to the depths of passion, from the joy of discovery to the heartache of loss, *Whispers Of The Heart* is a timeless tribute to the power of love and its ability to inspire and heal. Whether you're looking for a romantic escape, or simply in need of a reminder of the beauty of love, this book is sure to touch your heart and soul. So, take these poems to heart, and let them be a guide on your journey of love. And as you navigate the ups and downs of relationships and life, remember that love is not just a feeling, but a choice. A choice to put others first, to be patient and understanding, and to always have hope in the power of love.

Don't miss out!

Visit the website below and you can sign up to receive emails whenever FM Nickson publishes a new book. There's no charge and no obligation.

https://books2read.com/r/B-A-EMBY-UXFIC

BOOKS 2 READ

Connecting independent readers to independent writers.

Did you love *Echoes of Africatown: "Footprints of the ensalved"*? Then you should read *Whispers Of the Heart: Timeless Poetry*[1] by FM Nickson!

Love is a curious thing
    A paradox that weaves and clings.
    It's light as air, yet heavy as stone,
    It's sweet as honey, yet bitter when gone.
    It's a comfort and a challenge too,
    A force that can unite and tear apart, anew.
    It's the reason we live, and the cause of our strife,
    It's the greatest gift and the most painful knife.
    Love is both our savior and our doom,
    It can lift us up, or lead us to our tomb.
    It's the brightest star in the darkest night,
    It's the warmest embrace, and the coldest fright.

---

1. https://books2read.com/u/3nNerP

2. https://books2read.com/u/3nNerP

You must keep this book close, and return to it often, as a reminder of the beauty and wonder of love. Love is a journey, full of ups and downs, but through it all, its power abounds. It has the ability, to heal and inspire, and these carefully drafted poems are a testament, to its enduring fire.

For love is the foundation of a happy life, and it is a treasure that is meant to be cherished and nurtured.

About the Author

FM Nickson is a philanthropist, poet, historian, father, and founder of Meded Foundation, a non-profit organization that supports children suffering from sickle cell anemia with sponsored treatment and free education. In addition, he is also a published author, with works that include "Nemesis: The Last Sanctuary", Whispers Of The Heart, and "Echoes of Africatown," inspired by The Clotilda.